SKINNING OUT
—— TO SEA

BOWLINE BOOKS

Published in London by Bowline Books 2016
www.bowlinebooks.com

ISBN 978-0-9934295-0-7

SKINNING OUT —— TO SEA

by Mick Hugo

CONTENTS

INTRODUCTION
by Ken Worpole

In the 1960s, when Mick Hugo's account of his early life as a merchant seaman begins, Britain was a maritime nation and a maritime power. It had a large ship-building industry, an extensive fishing fleet, ports, docks and harbours busy with ships and workers, and a merchant navy that was, after the war, the largest in the world. All these factors combined to make sea-going and maritime work a crucial area of employment, and a significant contribution to British working class life and identity. When Hugo 'skinned out' to sea he was joining more than 150,000 other British merchant seamen then serving on ships across the world.

Joining the merchant navy was not just about finding a job. For many it was an escape – from boredom at school, from a difficult family situation, or even as a way of getting away from a brush with the law. For others, however, it represented an opportunity for travel and adventure, and for the author of this book it was clearly a combination of both. The merchant navy provided a safety valve for a lot of young men, enabling them to tear up their past and start again.

For this reason, perhaps, being a merchant seaman was not regarded as a particularly respectable occupation, though during the war the service had done phenomenally brave work, incurring a loss of more than 32,000 lives. This was never properly recognised, certainly not with the same significance as the losses of those serving in the armed forces, and only in recent times has this been rectified: Merchant Navy Day in September each year now commemorates this sacrifice.

As Mick Hugo recalls, life on board ship could be boring, uneventful and filled with petty routines, but it could also be hilarious as well as kindly. The odd assortment of seamen which the author encountered on each trip by necessity became, as he writes, 'your adopted family'. Yet the book reminds us that each ship was in its own way a sovereign state, with its officers empowered to bury people at sea, have crew members incarcerated, and able to enforce a chain of command that had the full weight of international law behind it. This strange mix of a command and control hierarchy, along with the 'live and let live' culture of the crew, must have been a difficult working environment to get used to. Members could not simply walk away – unless they jumped overboard as one of them did, in a chapter that the author very movingly and powerfully recalls.

The historian Rose George, in her recent and shocking study of the contemporary shipping industry, Deep Sea and Foreign Going (2013), paints a picture of an industry now so deregulated and shadowy in ownership, and often indifferent to the lives and conditions of its crew members, that it has become a global trade seemingly without principles or humanity. '*What happens at sea, stays at sea,*' George is told on several occasions when enquiring about a particularly unpleasant story of bullying or crew mistreatment.

'Skinning Out' tells a happier story on this occasion, enhanced by the author's own illustrations, which add a lovely touch to the narrative. Mick Hugo's wise and affectionate account of his early life at sea describes a more tolerant and better organised working life, when reasonable labour relations were taken seriously – though this was to change with the defeat of the 1966 Seaman's Strike. There are still too few accounts of the lives of those who worked at sea, and this book is all the more important for being such an engaging and gripping work of public memory and personal recollection.

SKINNING OUT

For some the nagging urge to flee your place of birth is an absolute.

Underlining post-school liberation was the need to put plenty of distance between me and the school gates, a stone's throw away and clearly visible from my bedroom window if it weren't for the recently erected – on the flattened site of the notorious "slum" dwellings of Essex Street – a high rise block of flats.

My limited options were compounded by having bunked off for most of the final year at school. How I'd become aware of and considered joining the merchant navy and the subsequent sea training course of deprivation with complete strangers, I don't know. There was no family history of going to sea and no one that I knew was or had been to sea. The nearest connection I had was occasionally in the dead of night, tucked up in bed, hearing the ships' hooters carried clearly on the wind as if the docks and the river Thames were at the bottom of the street. Now on reflection skinning out to sea was the perfect balance, placating wholesale flight with no real need to leave my village.

I managed to sail on eighteen ships in total including tiny coastal ships and a tanker, and almost always joined a ship when I was skint and bored. As with all my friends' parents, there was a shared post-war mentality, a pragmatic outlook that concentrated on the now, based not only on the hardships of the war years but also on the stark impoverishment of their upbringing that they had all endured. Ambition, if any, for their children was for them to be in work, regular work, no matter what it was, the priority above enlightened betterment was 'a wage'.

The years before the establishment of the welfare state were very raw for those at the bottom of the ladder. Areas like

Hoxton were hopeless poverty traps, prime examples of the worst of a class society.

I'm sure my mum (born 1909), as a product of those grim years, and ignoring her maternal instincts, had also seen, by me joining the Navy that I was escaping the mire and making good. My old man (born 1906) probably thought I was going off to war.

After first applying and being accepted for the merchant service on leaving school, I had to then wait until I was fifteen and a half, the legal age for recruitment. In the interim I was offered a job by the school 'careers officer', that was not the expected sweeping some crappy factory floor in Shoreditch, but as a messenger boy up West for a major film production company based in Chancery Lane. My stamping ground was mostly in and around Soho, a heady manor at that time, delivering and picking up film rushes and when idle escorting rather glamorous people through our labyrinth-like buildings to the studios. Thrust into this interesting environment almost turned my head, provoking the notion of whether to give the Navy lark business a miss or not. I'd also toward the end of my tenure been offered the opportunity to work as a trainee assistant editor. A perfect career beckoned, if only I'd recognised that at the time, while I just saw little stuffy cutting rooms – Sod that! I wanted horizons.

TRAINING SHIP VINDICATRIX

Having survived on occasion the desire to escape I am now feeling quite satisfied and proud that I held out. Departure day had finally arrived for me and my little group smartly attired in our sea trainee uniforms marching briskly to the main gates. Ten weeks of rudimentary seamanship tuition with orderly doses of square bashing had been completed. Representing 'the after' we encountered 'the before' – the incoming novices, rabbits caught up in the headlights, bewildered and bemused by the remarks hurled in their direction from the tight knowing unit passing them by pertaining to the nightmare that lay ahead. No doubt they themselves in ten weeks time would also be laying into the next batch of new recruits.

But first, awaiting them on crossing the threshold of Stalag 17 was a baptism of conformity, de-civilianising delivered by an odd ensemble of individuals, the welcoming committee, who were about to make their day with the stunned rabbits, relishing the torturers' power with well-worn remarks and jokes honed over many years on a multitude of innocents.

If you hadn't already by then turned, and had it on your toes back to the bosom of whatever part of the country you had come from, there instead would be compliant tittering and collective mirth from freshly shorn heads at the sight of the next fledglings to mount the chair to have their d/a's, elephant trunks, and sideburns – including my short little mod haircut, thought safe enough to pass muster – lopped off! Possibly by the local butcher from the nearby village, who rubbed his hands in the anticipation of extra cash subsidising the sale of tired sausages when a new contingency of fresh fodder arrived at the school gates. It could be a retrospective case for abuse, the tender delicate age when the process of individual preening begins, suddenly torn asunder.

Following the sheared sheep treatment there would be a cursory 'drop pants and cough'. After that, physical and medical check ups that included differentiating coloured symbols and letters, whereupon, to surprise and consternation, the odd one among us found that they were colour blind. A perceived career at sea on deck as first choice would instead become a career in the galley.

A visit to the camp store would be next, to be kitted out with the afore mentioned uniform plus sundry items not already requested to have been brought with you. Groups would then be formed and allocated to numbered billets uniformly placed within the camp enclosure adjacent to the wash-houses. Administrative buildings and stores congregated nearer the camp gates, and all were dominated by the central parade ground and recreation hall, the venue for the odd boxing bout releasing pressure with aggrieved inmates, keen to punch the lights out of each other.

The school hierarchy were housed in little brick houses on raised ground at a safe distance from the rabble.

Cooking, dining, and schooling took place on the retired old ship, the T. S. Vindicatrix, a once proud ocean-going three-master steam/ sailing ship now a dismasted, disabled relic permanently berthed in a canal-like tributary off the river Severn. Access was a short distance across a small lock bridge from the camp.

The billets, classic army/prisoner-of-war camp nissen huts, were lined with bunk beds and small personal lockers – invaluable when food parcels arrived from home. There were about twenty trainees crammed into each hut; at the entrance to the billet was a partitioned small room for the officer/instructor in charge of the group's welfare and discipline whilst in the billet. Daily instruction was given by a variety of tutors who – especially the long termers – were the usual nurtured quirky characters to be found in isolated regimes – rounded and bonkers.

The parting shot as we marched by the new recruits was a chorus or two of 'We wish you a merry Christmas' as their stint would include the Christmas period, but, with the words Christmas and New Year supplanted by – the perfectly rhyming – 'syphilis and gonorrhoea'. It seemed spontaneous at the time, started by a wit amongst us, but, no doubt was a regular naval take on the Xmas carol.

However, it made us feel that bit more mature than the newcomers. 'We knew what it was all about!' Ironically, us, the inexperienced, unsophisticated predominantly virginal 15-year-olds had only recently been given a pre-leaving lecture on the perils of the sex act and the consequences of such when in far-flung ports. Us, still awkward, spotty, and just about experienced in the odd snog, were taken through a graphic rickety slide show dominated by mutilated appendages by an odd looking bloke in an ill-fitting long white coat. 'The man from the ministry of VD?' His cheery parting retort was, 'Yes, a good majority of you will get the clap!'

To complete the assimilation we were issued with standard canvas kit bags to carry our belongings in, concealing any evidence of civilian entity, to go forth on discharge having satisfactorily completed the rigours designed to prepare us for a life at sea, or at least get through one trip. And, as in my case, report immediately that day to your nominated 'Pool' in said attire, as if that were the final act that completed the training.

THE POOL

'The Pool': the Labour Exchange for seamen situated in or around major ports in the British Isles. The KG5 (King George the Fifth) Pool was bang in the middle of the vibrant sprawling Royal Docks, in east London. Having journeyed that morning from the Gloucester-based sea training school by train, tube, then bus, I finally strode through the huge dock gates into a fascinating walled inner world of commerce, an awesome secret landscape. Vast constructed basins of water harnessed from the river Thames by a series of tidal locks. Warehouses, cranes, ropes, chains, capstans, crates, tugs, barges, cargo nets swaying with every array of cargo, loading and unloading, a whole chorus of human activity all there to service the magnificent ships now laying passive and motionless having arrived at varying intervals from all points of the world. I entered the pool, a low compact building just down from the dock gates with some trepidation, in uniform, carrying my sausage shaped kit bag, tie rebelliously loosened.

Once inside it didn't take long to realise – I should have gone home and changed! This place was the absolute opposite to the rigid formal environment I had just left behind. Outside, the dull winter grey of the docks and dockers, within milling around a colourful cast of pantomime characters, most tanned from their previous trips. Long hair, beards, shaven heads, tattoos, and earrings abounded, not yet quite de rigueur, especially for 1962 working class Inner London boys with their trim Perry Como haircuts and shiny box suits. Young middle-class college dwellers would slowly be venturing toward hippie attire, but not yet for the chaps – liberation from the rigid dress code of their manor would be slow to arrive.

So, here was I making my way through a faded denim clad milieu in my virgin uniform toward the counter – fortunately no one took the piss – and presented myself. Part of the processing on the day was to join the National Union of Seaman. Conveniently, the union bloke was sitting next to the Shipping Federation bloke, behind the counter, 'shoulder-to-shoulder, workmates?'

As a novice you are allocated your first ship, then for subsequent trips you are free to choose whatever ships are available. On one wall of the Pool office was a blackboard stretching the entire length, and on that board would be written the current jobs that were on offer – firstly the name of the ship and shipping company, then the number of crew required – deckhands – 2 ABS's, 3 EDH's, 1 JOS, deck boy, etc. – and the same for various different ratings for the catering and engine room departments. Then it would state the destination and length of journey. The latter would always be a bit ambiguous. Some ships were on regular runs and you knew to the day when you would be back, others may be diverted or arrive approximately around the time given, that could easily mean many weeks later. In theory when signing on ship's articles (a very binding agreement), you could be kept onboard for up to two years if the ship stayed away from British waters. The term 'Shanghaied' was used when unwittingly you were conned into joining such a ship, a practice that has now fortunately died out.

What was then taken for granted sadly will never be replicated. Footloose teenage lads if so disposed could enter the merchant service and find themselves looking up at that blackboard and pleasantly agonise as to what ship they may want to join, with every destination in the world on offer at one time or another. It could be careful daily consideration – until a ship and destination came up that you fancied – or simply, what ships in port and leaving first? Especially if skint, I could sign on today and get a small advance on wages. All as casual as you like. You could pay off one ship, stay ashore for as long as you liked, go back when you liked. The only requirement was to keep up with your union dues, a situation which changed after the bitter and long drawn-out Seamen's Strike of 1966, with the shipping companies tightening the knot restricting movement from company to company and drastically limiting time spent on shore leave.

A number of seamen hanging around the pool often stayed

at the local Seamen's Mission (The Flying Angel) if it was not their home port. In some cases the Mission and the ship were their only homes. Whatever their circumstances, they all inevitably went on the piss and would soon plough through their money, and, by degrees of avaricious consumption of drink, and peripheral generosity, soon would find themselves back on board the next ship, 'brassic' but safe.

Seamen's Missions were philanthropic and almost wholly Christian, set up to look after the welfare of seamen, providing a sanctuary in major ports all over the world offering bed, food, and a prayer, at a small cost.

My first trip was a short baptism of what I was going into. The ship, the Catalina Star of the Blue Star Line shipping company, had come into London from foreign trade and paid off the deep-sea crew. Then it was 'home trade' with the new crew to finally unload in Liverpool, short and sweet, not even two weeks. But, I still managed to be seasick before we were out of the Thames estuary. The ship, which was getting on in age, was buffeted the whole way up to Liverpool. My job as the complete rookie deck boy was to be the 'Peggy': that is to look after the deck hands' and greasers' Mess – the dining room – situated aft alongside the dark, grim, and compact accommodation. The galley, where the food was cooked, was mid-ships. I had the joy three times a day of making my way along the open decks, trying to keep upright in the wind and rain to collect the hot food in containers, and make it back to the Mess intact without mishap, and then present it ready to be served up at the allocated meal times. Not a pleasant task when feeling somewhat 'tom and dick' in an inescapable all-pervading environment of institutional cooking smells and debris-like food slopping around in accompaniment with the heaving seas. This led to the inevitable. Sympathetic deck hands, who've noticed that you are a little green in the gills, call out in unison, 'Oi, Peggy!' You turn around on unsteady feet, your ghostly complexion faces the smiling diners, and there they are smugly holding aloft between thumb and forefinger rashers of slimy, grease dripping bacon that's slowly entering their upturned mouths.

My trip to lovely Liverpool, though not as yet an exotic destination, was never the less a wide-eyed wonder, my first experience of another city other than London. The inhabitants had the same vibrancy as Londoners but with mad accents,

and everyone a comedian. The sprawling docks alongside Scotty Road went on forever. A world existed outside of London. I felt like a burgeoning explorer excited by all the possibilities and differences to come: this is on my doorstep, what is the rest to be like?

We had a night ashore before pay-off and jumping the train the following day back to London. There but for fate – having been taken along with some of the older lads to savour Liverpool night life, it was elected to visit the Iron Door Club for the evening, the decision made after espying a couple of rouged-up plump girls entering – so instead of the Cavern Club nearby, as yet not made famous but around that time featuring you know who, we missed a date with history.

Back in London there was a complete pea-souper, which extended for many days when you could not see a couple of feet in front of you. This delayed my venturing to the Pool for my next trip. The 'fate' that had deprived me of the kudos of maybe having seen the Beatles before fame had beckoned worked out kindly, with heavy fog delaying my return to sea for almost a week. It was quite possible that I could have joined a ship reasonably quickly and already been a few days out to sea, when on the eve of finally visiting the Pool I developed peritonitis and was whisked into hospital for an emergency operation.

Diagnosis and treatment at sea would have been non-existent. 'Brown bread at fifteen?'

OTAHEITE

It wasn't until after Christmas that I joined my next ship,
a complete opposite to my first. The passenger cruise liner,
Northern Star, embarking on a world cruise – whoa hey!
A three-month circumnavigation departing Southampton
in early January 1963 with ice on the ground, returning in late
March, there was still ice on the ground. I escaped the worst
winter in decades.

The first time that I got drunk memorably coincided
with when on the Northern Star tied up to the little dock of
Papeete, Tahiti. An awesomely beautiful part of the world.
A place still magical, making it so easy to understand and
imagine the experiences – though diluted by a couple of
centuries – that led twenty-one-year-old upper class Fletcher
Christian, Mate of the HMS Bounty, and his cohorts to go
native and mutiny. It must have seemed to the whole of the
crew, among who were some mangy specimens, that they had
arrived in heaven here on earth, an evocative South Sea Garden
of Eden. To most people the definitive image of paradise, even
despite a century of tourism from Gauguin to the now almost
daily visits of cruise ships. It still retains elements of the beautiful
life-style in a beautiful setting that must have seemed like the
modern day equivalent of dropping acid for the men of the
Bounty – the conditions in late eighteenth-century Britain, for
the majority of the ship's crew and their class, would have been
complete purgatory.

The short dip into this paradise was but for a day and night
as is the case for passenger cruise ships gobbling up cultures for
their over-fed cargo. The hardly concealed excitement of the
untravelled novice youngsters of the crew was heightened
somewhat when observing the free and easy young Tahitians
diving and swimming from the harbour side. It was a bit of a

sideshow for the passengers who threw money into the crystal-clear blue water that was deftly retrieved as it glided under by the young brown amphibious bodies.

Not to be outdone, during a work-break a collection of deck and stewards boys raised the flag for blighty and entered the water. Our lily-white bodies, in unflattering baggy shorts not then fashionable, clambered over the bow and precariously onto the mooring ropes. Where upon we in a fashion jumped, fell off, belly flopped and dive-bombed with a mad inelegant energy. Probably, not far removed from that of the afflicted crew of the Bounty, when sighting the smiling, waving, bare breasted apparitions paddling their flower adorned canoes toward the anchored ship.

After the boisterous enthusiasm in the mid-day sun, perhaps thinking we had matched cool with cool having gained some applause from the passenger decks, surprisingly our unconventional display did not bring a ticking off from our superiors, but just a touch of sunburn. This meant for my little fair-skinned self that the combination of a touch of sunburn with the coming evening's rite of passage into the consumption of alcohol was not the perfect preparation for my inauguration into the world of altered states. At least that was my excuse for my remembered behaviour.

The evening ended only after a shipmate and I on borrowed bicycles collapsed in a heap in the middle of the road and were subsequently escorted back to the ship by a burly Tahitian policeman who pretty much with one hand on each of us raised us up off the ground and gave us a friendly lecture on why we should not be riding other people's bicycles. It was a sobering moment. Otherwise I feel that once horizontal, unconsciousness would have soon followed.

Having got safely back onboard, but not to my cabin, I flaked out on the very top deck of the liner which happened to be the passenger games deck – a no-go area for crew. Possibly my mindset after I got there may have been to sleep under the stars and not in the labyrinth-like bowels of the ship, but more likely that I was due to go on duty that night as bridge boy and collapsed in a stupor before I got there. But, in my condition nothing mattered, even when I was being prodded and kicked by the Fourth Mate who obviously, as he was the duty officer on watch, would have been apoplectic to have found a lowly deck boy sprawled out on his patrolled passenger territory and more so when the deck boy was telling him to 'fuck off!'

There was a bit of a history between us. It was during the beginning of the trip as bridge boy and milling about the wheelhouse I was told at some point to stand out on the wing of the bridge. This was my first proper deep-sea trip so I was not as yet steeped in the wiles of what it is to be a seaman. I aimlessly stood around. After a while the first spots of rain began to fall, so, I came into the enclosure of the bridge and stood there as idly as I was on the wing that was open and exposed to the elements.

It was then the diminutive Fourth Mate, bolt upright and rigid, in his slightly oversized stiffly-pressed uniform, bore down upon me. There were other officers on the bridge that didn't seem to care where I was, given my status as an apprentice deck hand with no role in the workings of the bridge and whose usefulness was confined to the endless job of polishing the collection of brass and copper navigation lamps in the lamp room tucked behind the bridge. And running errands.

'What are you doing in the wheelhouse? You haven't been told to come in?'

'It's just started to rain,' I answered.

'Rain!?'

'Yea! It's just started.'

'Get back out there! This minute!'

I am unsure that he hasn't heard me right. 'It's raining – I'll get wet.'

'WET! WET! Get out onto the wing of the bridge now!'

'No!'

'What did you say?'

'No! If I go out there I'm gonna get wet,' still hoping he may get the logic of what I am saying. But no, he hadn't as he came closer, face to face and said slowly in his most commanding voice that erred toward the falsetto.

'GET!... OUT!... THERE!... NOW!'

I was not fully absorbed into this authoritarian lark, and not yet appreciative that getting wet and putting up with all sorts of weather was the deck hand's lot. By now I was feeling a little bit irked by this unjust outburst. It was now pissing down and I wasn't going to stand in heavy rain for no apparent reason.

'Na' fuck off! I'm not!'

This provoked a wide-eyed blank stare from the Fourth Mate and silence while his mind raced as to what to do next. Fortunately for me the Second Mate, who was an alright bloke, was present and had overheard our exchanges and may have been mildly amused by the standoff (I don't think he was overly fond of the Fourth Mate). He intervened.

'Hugo! It's time to pick up our sandwiches. Lively, I'm starving.'

Off I go in a flash, internally through the accommodation, keeping nice and dry, leaving the Fourth Mate staring into the space that I'd occupied.

Nothing came of it. I could have been logged and fined for my insubordination, if I had been anything other than a first tripper and hadn't had the timely intervention of a senior officer who nipped the escalating confrontation in the bud. So on that wonderful night in paradise, a couple of furtive kicks from the Fourth Mate and a few fuck-offs from me ended with him wandering off and leaving me to it, but also reporting me, and I being duly logged.

To be logged meant to be reprimanded for breaking rules that covered a spectrum of misdemeanours including being late or failing to turn up for work or duty. Details were formally entered into the Ship's Log alongside the punishment meted out by the ship's master. There was very little room for manoeuvre and hardly ever a slap on the wrist. Once you were reported the inevitable fines were dished out, amounting to forfeiting a day's pay, increasing in the number of days subject to the perceived severity. Quite often the pettiness of some loggings suggested – not only to the cynical – that it was wholly favourable to the shipping companies. The more loggings the less wages to be paid.

THE INTERMENT

The Northern Star belonged to the Shaw Saville Shipping Company and had a sister ship, the Southern Cross, both reasonably new ships carrying 1,000 passengers apiece. They had inherited, along with 'leisure cruising' for some, the task of continuing the transportation of migrants to Australia. This was a scheme promoted throughout the nineteen-fifties and early sixties, encouraged by the Australian government to bulk out its colony. This scheme was heavily subsidised, with émigrés having to pay a nominal fee of ten pounds to willingly go where once early colonials were forcibly transported. Now a dream new life in the sun beckoned. After first severing ties with family, friends, and country of birth, they journeyed into the unknown to the opposite end of the earth to be then plonked into grim hostel/holding camps (whilst they got over the shock and managed to get on their flip flopped feet) in the somewhat strange and hostile terrain of a vast continent. Brave stoic souls. These passengers were always referred to as 'ten-pound stowaways'.

For some, on board for a cruise, no future beckoned: death and burials at sea were not uncommon. Elderly passengers on last gasp cruises would often be zapped into a state of near-pneumonia by the ship's sometimes vicious air conditioning. Maybe, there is one of those naughty websites out there giving advice to carers and would-be benefactors. What you need to do is take dear old Auntie Maud on deck in the sun for a prolonged period, preferably around midday, and when you feel yourself perspiring say, 'Nap time!' Then hurtle her as fast as possible back into the fridge of a cabin – you may have to repeat this exercise over a period of days.

The procedure for a burial at sea was that the deceased would be sewn into a canvas body-bag, along with two heavy weights made especially for the task of taking the average body to the bottom of the ocean. Once official certification of death is made – the logistics, where in the world, how many days away from land, and what onboard facilities there were for keeping a body preserved for a prolonged period. This, if it were possible, equalled lots and lots of money to bring dear old Auntie Maud back to a twee little English county crematorium to be incinerated, and did not make economic sense. So, the decision made by loving families for what seemed like an archaic burial is made, and is being made around this time, somewhere in the world.

Being a very big ship one of the several deck boys was assigned to the Lamp Trimmer. The term 'lamp trimmer' was born of old when lamps were lit and wicks were trimmed, and the person responsible evolved into the keeper of the stores whose duties were dishing out whatever was necessary for deck maintenance. He was a skilled seaman who undertook repairs to running parts of deck equipment, and when required was expected to undertake tasks such as splicing the mooring ropes, as well as the back springs, which were made of wire. He could be tight or generous when handing out tools or materials to the crew, generally erring toward the tight, thus giving the impression that it was his personal property you were receiving – even the rag bag would be under strict control.

The 'rag bag', a by-product of the rag trade, contained old clothing finally deemed unrecyclable, gaining a few pennies more as rags for cleaning. The interesting thing about the humble rag bag was its ability to transcend itself from its lowly status in the fo'csle store – a weird take maybe. But diving into the rag bag was like stirring up multiple histories, all the varying pieces of clothing once a part of a garment proudly adorned, a corner stone of civilisation requiring people 'to be well dressed and smartly turned out'. When coming across a particular pretty feminine piece of material, that throughout the relegation process still retained the perfume of its wearer, the urge to close your eyes and thrust your nose head long into it taking an abnormally long sniff is irresistible, yes, and sad. The mitigating circumstances are that you have been at sea for some time, are in an all-male environment, you are up to your neck in some crappy job on a windswept deck, and before you know it just as you are about to use your rag to mop up some spillage. So you go – wallop! And bury your head in the rag.

The Lamp Trimmer's boy assisted the lampy throughout the voyage. This was generally regarded as a cream job with not much to do. But back to death at sea. The canvas body-bag, weights, twine, palm and needles were collected from the store by a grizzled old Able Seaman who would not have looked out of place on the set of a spaghetti western. He eagerly volunteered to do the deed as he had done in the past, for in payment for his services he got the day off work and a bottle of whisky, which he all but finished before completing the task. Whilst sewing away he held court with anyone passing by the open upper deck locker, the venue for dead body sewing, and when no one was around for a chat he was overheard singing to his charge. The Lamp Trimmer was not present when the necessary bits were collected, so the lamp trimmer's boy and the old Able Seaman between them sorted out the requisite materials.

When the time came, the funeral service took place on the after deck. A form of chute was erected on the after rail, and at the time of committal to the sea, the body bag, draped with the Red Ensign, would be cut loose and slide unencumbered down the chute away from the ship's side and enter the wake for a perfect ten. Family mourners, if any, would congregate alongside the other inquisitive passengers. Unless there happened to be a ship's chaplain on board, the captain would read the necessary service, fellow officers from different departments would also attend all in their finest tropical white uniforms dripping with yellow braid, a sombre occasion.

The Lamp Trimmer who had been missing for most of the day arrived back at the fo'csle stores and discovered that the rusty old weights that had been lingering in a dark corner of the store were still there, and the brand new shiny weights recently taken on board were missing. In his slight intoxicated state (the reason he'd been absent for most of the day) and his natural miserly tendencies, it was far too much for him to take. The Lamp Trimmer's boy got a torrent of abuse for allowing the brand new shiny items to be taken and for his bemused response – 'A weight is a weight' – almost a whack round the ear from a quivering raised hand of the enraged lampy. He then witnessed the big lump of a beer-bellied lamp trimmer sweep up the rusty old heavy weights under each arm and with a glazed look in his eyes take off down the decks blissfully unaware as to what stage the proceedings were at. Weaving in and out of startled passengers, in between puffing and panting, was heard to be saying 'Stop! Stop! Wrong weights!'

Fortunately the decks were long, possibly a circuit would be a half a mile for the fitness wallahs. Lampy was far from fit and the weights got the better of him, he petered out just when he was about to be in earshot of the mourners. The evident realisation that his shiny new weights were about to enter the drink, he sheepishly turned round avoiding complete embarrassment, and hauled his rusty weights back through the smattering of passengers still lingering on the decks, they all viewed him cautiously. The Lamp Trimmer's boy hid for the rest of the day.

SUD AMERICA

The Arlanza, a cargo passenger ship belonging to Royal Mail Lines, was one of three sister ships including the Amazon, which I also sailed on, as well as the Aragon. They were on regular 6 – 7 week runs to South America. The itinerary was, outward bound, depart London–Boulogne–Vigo–Lisbon–Las Palmas, then a nine day crossing to Rio de Janeiro–Santos–Montevideo–Buenos Aires, stay for ten days then homeward bound, stopping again at the same ports as outward but adding Southampton, then finally London, a neat little itinerary for that short period of time.

The ships carried 1st, 2nd and 3rd-class passengers who were confined to designated areas of the ship away from the cargo hatches and the nasty rough seamen. 1st class inhabited the upper decks, 2nd class the mid decks, and 3rd class were positioned on the lower and after decks, naturally! I had the cushy number of 1st class games deck boy under the wing of a senior Able Seaman who had the even cushier token job of being in charge of the smooth running of the 1st class decks and putting me, his assistant, to work. He protected his most sought-after job from usurpers from the AB ranks by ruling with a rod of iron. He even threatened to fill me in, 'the mere boy', when I once, with good reason, contradicted him.

He strutted his preening self around the decks in clean crisp whites with a constant predatory eye poised for an opportunity to pull. He was no great shakes, so am not sure of his success rate if any. The man who held this crown was the swimming pool attendant and part-time masseur, now slowly approaching over the hill status. He was no doubt, when young, a handsome Latin-looking chap, though I think he originated from Rochdale. Now his black skimpy Speedo's displayed a fleshy overhang, and his hair looked unnaturally blacker than black, but his bronzed torso and well-honed charm still attracted female attention and clients for the massage table.

The smell of scented wealth and Ambre Solaire on those privileged decks was evocative. What a job the swimming pool attendant had! He even went off, having nothing to do, for the whole time that we were in Buenos Aires, obviously, the bastard was servicing and mixing it with his rich connections that he had compiled over the years.

Meanwhile in anonymity I sweated over my various tasks, an occasional voyeur to the frivolity of the sun-kissed First Class decks, and the sexually charged coterie around the swimming pool. Like the servile butler observing all, saying nothing, a piece of the furniture, no way a part of the action.

Well... One day while busying myself sorting the deck games box, a voice piped up behind me, a European-accented English female voice asking me for the deck quoits. It was a girl that I had definitely noticed, about my age 16 – 17. A small conversation struck up on how best to throw and play deck quoits, and she lingered a little longer than necessary, both afflicted with shy smiles, and awkward now after I had exhausted the vagaries of deck quoits technique. She turned to rejoin her family group.

The ship's crew was forbidden to fraternize with the passengers (pool attendant accepted), over and above what was necessary for those working on the passenger decks. Officers could, and were encouraged with discretion to attend to passengers' social needs. My fleeting contact, as minuscule as it was, was exciting enough to put a frisson into my humble lot. I looked out for her the following day. We exchanged more shy smiles and hellos, the next day a few words and names. I was high; Gaby was from Switzerland travelling to Buenos Aires to visit family.

We soon shared the need for discretion when our meetings and chats became more frequent in the claustrophobic confines of the decks. Her, for her strict chaperoning parents, and me 'the forbidden' who was beginning to receive glares from my boss, who was probably no more than jealous that I was making some sort of contact and he had not. It soon became just a matter of days before the ship would be arriving in Buenos Aires, Gaby's destination. We talked of meeting up of an evening when darkness fell and the coast would be clearer, and we knew this would be impossible in the small intimate environment of the upper class decks. We daringly decided to meet in the 3rd class area of the ship and mingle in with the 'poor passengers' sitting around and taking the evening air on the after decks.

We made it. Gaby managed to get away from her parents, whose turn it was to be dining at the Captain's table, and made her way through the upper decks and I made my way via the lower decks and crew quarters. Gaby was lovely, cultured and attractive, and had a brace on her teeth. We talked. Kissed, talked and kissed. It was a beautiful two hours together, snuggled up on the after-deck, watching the meandering moonlit wake, and we parted reluctantly, Gaby had been out of sight for far too long. The ship was due to stay in port for a longish period; Gaby gave me the phone number of the house that she would be staying at with her family in Buenos Aires. Tied up in BA, we were keen to meet up. I rang the number that Gaby gave me, and a male answered in what I assumed was Argentinean. I blurted out thoroughly nervous:

'May I speak to Gaby please?'

'Who? Who is this? What do you want?'

'Can I speak to Gaby please?'

Aggressively the voice answered; 'Why do you want to speak to Gaby? WHO ARE YOU?'

I hung up. Having no answers that would make him say, 'Oh, hold on a moment and I'll get her for you.' The following day I just about summoned up the courage to ring again. A male voice answered. The same voice!

I hung up.

Foiled. Inevitably we would not see each other again, confined now to a fleeting memory of the briefest of shipboard encounters. Sad, but some ways relieved, it would have been totally traumatic to have managed to have clandestinely met. The spectre of her father leaping out on me (a duck out of water), screaming 'Who are you!?' would surely have panicked me into cowardly 'having it away on my toes', and taking off at full pelt without a backward glance.

Recovery from my grand unrequited romance was helped by being launched into the underbelly of Buenos Aires – where my class properly belonged – with my ship mates: young naïve lambs to the slaughter, managing not to be wholly sacrificial by the presence of older members of the ship's company ashore cavorting in the same clubs and bars.

Among the older shipmates was a fellow Londoner, Able Seaman Lenny Butcher – a handsome bastard, his classic tanned, chiselled features topped with tousled blond hair stood him out among the crowd. A cockney from Bow, from a family associated with working on the Thames. One more generation on would have made him taller than he was, not helped by a slightly bow-legged inheritance out for a last showing from an ancestry of under-nourished working class Londoners. A developed torso that didn't deserve its legs passed on through the genes and maintained with hard labour and not the gym, strong, wiry and often exposed at the drop of the sun, a glowing example of the deficiency in physical symmetry of some of the crew. He was the 'Billy Budd' among men, liked by all for his extrovert chirpy humour and laissez-faire. He had so much going for him with looks and personality one wondered why he had been going to sea for so long and not cashed in somewhere.

The bar of choice that all ranks gravitated to as the evening wore on was seedily plush and jumping. At one corner of the dance floor and perched on a small stage was a very alive band pumping out fantastic Latin sounds interjected with the odd well-known pop tune of the day. There was a healthy level of male to female revellers equalling the also healthy level of visiting seafarers to local members of the public out for an evening of fun, and it was slightly above the clip joints and dives inhabited by en-suite hostesses and shady chancers that dotted the red light district. It had the feel of a genuine public venue. In places like this getting pissed was elevated to an exotic level, a more relishing of the intoxicating ambience that was heady rather than legless, if a distinction can be made.

It was at that lovely moment in time when you hadn't yet started slurring your words and beginning to talk bollocks – you know that moment – when, into the club entered Lenny Butcher with a small predominantly female entourage, and Claudia Cardinale on his arm – well, not exactly, but it may as well have been. She was a stunning beautiful woman, a ringer for the Italian actress.

Lenny spotted us young flushed chaps and with his dazzling entourage was over to join our company full of bonhomie. Managing not to faint with this now intimate association with these ladies and noticing the young steward's boys looking on – our peer group competition – we felt like the coolest dudes in town. It wasn't long within this dream place when suddenly upon the stage without notice jumped Lenny Butcher! And

never got chucked back off – they just must have known him
from previous trips. He proceeded to take the evening by storm,
subjugating the band's singer to a welcomed rest. Could he sing,
the bastard with everything except straight legs. He wowed the
crowds and kept banging out the songs with, among others,
Trini Lopez numbers that were current in the hit parades at that
time 'If I Had a Hammer' – a numero uno.

How odd, how proud, this fellow cockney English man giving it to them in Buenos Aires. I could just imagine this sing-song pub somewhere in Bow, where the Butcher clan bee-lined to on a Saturday night and taking off when the young Lenny was home on shore leave.

Not quite an adult, this meant that there was no resentful envy that no doubt his peer group could not help but feel on occasion. But pure admiration, alpha male charisma on display, effortlessly pulling women like Claudia Cardinale, reflective glory because you know him, and 'yea that's gonna be me one day.' Youthful thoughts, but alas – oh well! I don't remember getting back to the ship, but I'm sure me and my buddies blew our cool and got into the inevitable drunken mess.

It was after Buenos Aires – I don't recall it as a sudden revelation or it being a complete surprise – but my fellow cockney, one of your own, Lenny boy, turned out to be having a long-term relationship with... the ship's captain's steward. 'What!? A bloke? What about Claudia?' Expecting presumed heterosexual teenagers to take things on board, is not far removed from expecting a one-year-old to run before it can walk. The ambiguity of sexual orientation then was probably confined to an abstraction that hung in the air like that of a pantomime dame, various slang references abounded in general rhetoric for homosexuals, when the word 'gay' meant to be happy. The only one brave real-life queer – old money terms – to every one's knowledge in my manor was Diamond Lil, who inhabited pubs in Bethnal Green, and whose outrageous queen behaviour and furtive activity with big bad East End tough guys confirmed Lil's celebrity status.

The bigger ships of the Merchant Navy at the time were a haven to those not yet out from the closet. This particular ship was a passenger cargo with a large number of crew. You could go through a whole trip and not encounter a good proportion of the crew. So some things were not ever secret – they just did not emerge. I suppose I must have been a bit taken aback. I mean he was a proper bloke, nothing like a mincing Diamond Lil or an innuendo-ridden Frankie Howerd – nothing stereotypical just an ordinarily acting bloke who could pull with ease Claudia Cardinale. What a waste, I mean what – mindset at the time – what could Billy Budd see in a bloke, and a skanky geezer of a steward to boot. It turned out sometime later that the skanky steward was far from skanky, and very much an equal, though with opposite qualities to Lenny – handsome, urbane, sophisticated, a really nice bloke. Someone who with ease also could have pulled Claudia Cardinale.

THE HINAKURA

The New Zealand Shipping Company was not such a well liked outfit to work for, but their ships were on an extremely well-liked run. The trip to Kiwi was a must for all lusty youngsters, a guaranteed destination to lose your cherry. Local girls were attracted to foreign ships; it was akin to a small somewhat boring village where young interesting visitors turned up regularly to party. The good times had when in Kiwi contributed to a high incidence of seamen jumping ship, heads turned by romantic liaisons and a naivety that the party would continue after their ship had departed. The reality of their 'joie de vivre' inevitably quickly turning sour when money ran out, being dobbed in and rounded up quite easily in the relatively small communities.

As un-luck would have it, on my first exclusively Kiwi trip I had no chance to party or consider jumping ship, as on the first somewhat raucous night ashore for the crew in the small town of New Plymouth, after weeks at sea, I managed to get myself nicked. I spent the night in the local police station, and the following morning found myself being transferred to New Plymouth prison where I was to be kept on remand until I came up in court. It was a reasonably high security prison, housing lifers among its inmates. The prison was situated in the small town for the impregnability of its position, surrounded by sea and mountains. If prisoners broke out they would not have got far. This sentiment prevailed still and was borne out whilst I was there.

There was a full front page report in the local newspaper, accompanied by graphics with dots and arrows, of the route taken by two recent escapees. They had been members of a trusted work party renovating skylights via scaffolding on the prison roof. The two were cell mates and had discreetly – after discovering the skylight that serviced their own cell – contrived, according to the report, to leave theirs open at the end of the day's work. The route indicated they had made their way out after lockdown through the skylight and down the scaffold and, aided by scaffold ladders, traversed the prison's inner and outer walls. The graphic arrows continued to zig-zag through some neighbouring streets, ending at an off-license which they promptly broke into and spent some time consuming drink. The marked route then returned along the same line, scaled the walls and scaffolding, and popped back into the skylight. They had loaded themselves down with carry outs of varying bottles of spirits and bulging pockets of fags, leaving a trail of items along the way in the unsteady scramble to continue their session back in their cell. It was stated that they felt in their drunken state that their little wheeze would not be discovered, so they could repeat similar excursions again at a later date. Unfortunately the scene the following morning that confronted the screw on opening the cell door blew their little secret. Two unconscious prisoners stinking of booze, amid piles of full and emptied bottles, cartons of fags and a wide open skylight.

Not a good time for me either. It would be a while until the court came to town. From the round hole in the door a mouth was summoning me, in broken English, a mouth, which on closer inspection had not seen much dental attention.

'Hey! Hey! You seaman ya?'

'Yea!'

'I seaman too...'

'Oh yea!'

'What you in for?'

'I wait go home, get deported.'

'Oh, why's that?'

'I miss ship, get big trouble. I wait next German ship, then go home.'

The mouth with discoloured and missing teeth did not quite marry up with the image of a clean-cut German national. Just the mouth filled the hole, no nose, no eyes, no face, just a talking cell door. I volunteer, eager in my isolation to communicate with a fellow being;

'I'm in a bit of trouble too, am on remand until I come up in court.'

'Vot you do?'

'Oh, lots!,' I answered sheepishly, not realising that that one question would produce a sick helpless feeling, taking me straight back to the reality of my present situation that the little pile of Reader's Digest's I'd been ploughing through and consoling myself with had momentarily taken me away from.

'Sorry! You be OK, You got cigarettes?'

'No!'

'Here I give you.' A couple of skinny roll-ups and a part of a book match were passed through the hole.

'Thanks, thanks!'

'OK, got to go, I see you.' The mouth disappeared along with the arrival of clanking boots on the landing. A fag at last - I'd been gasping.

The mouth belonged to Karl and arrived daily at the same time, always fleetingly and accompanied with a few skinny rollups. I was so grateful to this generous stranger – smokes were precious – and comforted by not feeling totally alone. Sharing my plight with a fellow seaman lessened the gravity just a tiny little bit. I tell myself – I'll be all right, seamen get banged up all the time around the world – to make me feel better, and somehow normalise my predicament. But it doesn't last long, and leaden despair drops in rather lively until brief respite once more, after another plunge into a heart-warming, feel-good stories in the well thumbed Reader's Digests. My little tatty pile of drugs on tap, I reckon, getting me out of my predicament for the duration of the stories. How I had sneered when the screw said, 'Here you are, some books to read.'

A big relief was being allowed out into the courtyard, and open air, in the mornings and afternoons, and especially when I was later to be joined in the yard by a fellow remandee, a whole person to communicate with – instead of just a decaying mouth – for brief moments.

The enclosed courtyard was approximately 30 metres by 15 metres. At one end, overlooking the yard, was a reception area, with people coming and going, and manned by a trustee prisoner and a current duty prison officer. You got the feeling that the trustee ran the show with an autistic knowledge, as result of it being the sum total of his world of numbers, forms, procedures. An efficient prissy, overweight, salacious-looking character who may have been doing this prized prison job, segregated from the rest of the inmates and prison routine, for his own safety. But, more likely, it was for the safety of the rest of the prisoners. He had an air about him of the Hannibal Lector. And often, because of the lack of activity in reception, he would be sitting at the window leering out at those remandees in the yard. He may well have been being ultra efficient, prematurely sizing up individuals for prison garb, anticipating the weighing up and sentencing of the hapless remandees. But for me it looked like 'what limbs would he sever first?'

At the opposite end of the yard, in the middle of the wall in the slightest of recesses – no cubicle, no door, no privacy, totally exposed and totally opposite the reception room window – was an outside toilet. Of a morning the choice was; cell or yard – whatever you chose, that was it for the day. I pretty much had self-imposed constipation for the whole period of my incarceration. I was never much good at crapping in strange places, but with Hannibal's 'boat-race' peering through the window I totally clamped up before even ever considering trying. A wee I could manage, but not without making sure there was no face at the window when I chose my moment.

Hannibal's presence though was relegated to inconsequence when I was joined by my fellow-remandee, a life-affirming character by the name of Neville Teehoo. Neville was a tough-looking Maori, and was forever getting into scrapes and getting himself nicked. We were both due up in court on the same day, he was expecting to go away and he thought I had a good chance too. Something I didn't quite want to hear, but he reassured me that it would be great! Neville was experienced enough to know his fate with regard to the charges against him, and was confident and looking forward to another spell in an open prison somewhere in the countryside, where he could take up again and use his skills in distilling gin. Apparently they were easy-going places.

Because of his pragmatic outlook and knowledge of the system, a little time inside was regarded as a holiday, some time off from the stress of the outside. He probably thought I would like his verdict – on hearing of my misdemeanours – that I was likely to go down. No thanks! I belong on the other side of the world. I didn't want to be banged up in some skanky prison, open or not, drinking 150 proof gin mixed with piss for the aberration of one night's revelry and taking the rap for all the wrong-doings on that first night ashore. I was a bit worried though. Anyway, the hours pacing the yard was the good part of the day with Neville's amusing stories of his life and things that he had got up to. He was no way a bad person, a really nice gentle bloke who'd become firmly labelled by his exuberance, as well as being marginalised as a Maori at the bottom end of the ladder, with a destiny of a life in and out of trouble, and then prison, always beckoning.

My day in court arrived. I was escorted on foot by two very large policemen. Being a small town, the court was not far from the prison. I felt awkward in the midday sun, a felon between burly upholders of the law strolling toward the courthouse along a dusty high street among locals going about their business. Then it was up onto the raised timber boardwalk and into the court, and finally the shade, escorted into a side room off the main court, where I was reunited with Neville in his best and in no doubt only patched up suit and tie, his attire no doubt insisted upon by the ample presence of his mum.

She was weary, helplessly dignified, doing what mothers have done forever, supporting their offspring, the once-upon-a-time gurgling bonnie babies at their breast. Good boys and girls who have now fallen foul, with the solemnity of age, some trapped unluckily in a lineage of the down trodden, others unfathomably nasty pieces of work. They remain still beautiful babies, innocent in a mother's eye, who may just concede, 'perhaps they could be a little bit naughty at times.'

I came up first. If I weren't so freaked out I would have felt totally embarrassed as six charges were read out, accompanied six times with 'Do you want to be charged in this court, and if so, how do you plead?' Six times I said, 'This court!' Six times, 'Guilty!' The nature of the charges I did not quite take in. I wanted it over with. I did notice though that the final charge was of being 'a rogue and vagabond?' I was fined for each charge and, to my great relief, there was no mention of a custodial. The ship was in port for the whole period of my detention, which seemed like forever, but was for just over one week. I rejoined it within a day of its scheduled sailing – another relief.

I'd heard that the Captain could have bailed me out at the very beginning, but decided not to. A lesson for my benefit to be learnt, maybe? No, he was a bastard, and would have happily left my little distressed self there to rot. It was a fluke that I came up in court a day before the ship sailed. I can't quite remember having been in a contrite Catholic state of mind, of bring on the punishment. It would not have been a surprise that I was also logged and fined for being missing for the period of time. What I did know was that after a small allotment sent home, and after paying some small debts, I was paid off that ship after a four-month trip with twelve pounds.

Homeward bound on the Hinakura was highlighted by the following logging-related occurrence that a half a century later rates as one of my proudest moments.

A head peered around my cabin door and hissed in hushed tones; 'He's out for the count!'

'What!? Well out?'

'Well out! Pissed and flaked out in the chart room.'

Yes! The time had come. The Second Mate had done it again. I hadn't quite expected that the request made to the incoming watch-keeper when watches rotated recently would be relayed so eagerly. Tacit approval and a keenness for what I was plotting was evident on his face – not a fan of the soon-to-be victim. I couldn't bail out now. It was coming toward the end of the 8 – 12 watch, and I was now on day work and had no right to be contemplating roaming about on the bridge at that time of the night, but, the conditions were right. I minded again why I was set on some kind of mission of revenge. So, instead of bottling out I was up and moving, not much time before change of watch.

I found the necessary implements, my chosen weapon, and was out onto the dark decks and up the ladders connecting the main deck to the wheelhouse, heart thumping. I nervously slid open the wheelhouse door. 'What am I doing?' I entered on automatic and began to cross the darkened floor toward the shaft of light coming from the chartroom. I listened intently as I quietly crept forward, there were no sounds of activity. I slowly peered through the doorway into the brightly lit chartroom. And there he was, in the same condition as on a few occasions previously. He liked his gin and the long watch would often get the better of him. Then, when found, the lookout would revive him in time for the next officer of the following watch to arrive and relieve him.

So, it had come as a great surprise, that I, I who had on more than one occasion, whilst on the same watch as he, saved his bacon and the embarrassment of being discovered asleep on duty by a fellow officer, was whilst blissfully working away on deck one morning approached by the Bosun, who informed me that I'd been summoned to the Captain's cabin to be logged on a charge of lying down on lookout the previous evening; not sleeping, but lying down? Lookout was kept on the fo'csle head in view of the bridge. The practice with all lookouts was that you could manage because of the configuration of the fo'csle to sit down if you fancied and be as vigilant still with a clear view and duly report lights that had popped up on the horizon even though we were in the middle of the Indian Ocean and hadn't seen any shipping for days.

I was incensed that this drunken sop of a Second Mate, the man who was in supreme control and totally responsible for the safety of the ship whilst duty officer, would actually flake out unconscious and then have the bollocks on one comparatively sober night to blearily scan the fo'csle with his binoculars and notice the lookout was not bolt upright and report him for failing in his duty. No amount of protest had any effect – I was logged and fined. I felt like grassing up the smug bastard standing red-eyed and furtive behind the captain who was seated at the table where 'justice' was meted out, though it would have fallen on deaf ears. It was immediately then that I plotted, or rather more realistically fantasized revenge. As fate would have it the old lush would flake out again at a convenient moment and present me with the opportunity.

The tropical uniform, white shoes, white full-length socks, stiffly pressed white baggy shorts and white short-sleeved shirt, laying there inhabited by the skinny runt of a Second Mate, third in line of importance in a British Merchant vessel, the prime of Officer class, scourge of the lower orders throughout history, flat on his back on the chartroom bench, out of it. There could not have been a better opportunity to dole out some form of poetic justice. Out came my tin, lid off, cloth folded into a pad. Tentatively I began to apply the black boot polish, first his exposed upper legs, he never flinched, then a little bolder as much as I could get to on both bare arms. There was slight movement and a faint expelling of air that sent me rigid. I rationalized, if he did wake up it would be somewhat laboured, before his drunken eyes opened and focused I could be away and out of sight. If however, I considered somewhat later, if he had awoken suddenly and caught me in the act, I had done so much already that it would have presented him with a dilemma. However, I thought; 'fuck it, let's go the whole hog', and proceeded to apply the boot polish to his face in a gingerly fashion and managed to complete his black and white minstrel look without dragging him out of his drunken sleep. I stood back and admired my work, turned and quietly departed almost choking with the effort it was taking trying to stifle the urge to maniacally cackle. I was in no time back to my cabin and turned in indulging with much pleasure and satisfaction before descent into sleep. Imagining over and over again the moment his relief arrived and confronted the situation before him. I also not so boldly had panicky ears open in case there was a commotion as a result – nothing! And, nothing the following day, and not an inkling for the rest of the trip – a near as perfect, having one over on the stiff pompous git. And absolutely no comeback.

The cargo ship Cuzco, belonging to the Pacific Steam and Navigation Company, sailing from London stopping at various ports in the West Indies, Venezuela, Panama, Ecuador and Peru. This whole evocative part of the world has always been a magnet, a complete antithesis to Britain, despite its repressive bloody history, its dictatorships, the shanties, the poverty, the uninhibited nature of the inhabitants – a beacon for early day 'Brits abroad'. Somehow any mayhem that may have ensued as result of visiting crews was looked upon leniently; 'they spent money'. And if there were any over-stepping of the mark there was always the shipping company rep or British consulate official who could intervene and save them from possible incarceration.

There were some who embraced this part of the world more than others. One such character, who also happened to be the Lamp Trimmer of the Cuzco, was distinct from the rest of the crowd... He'd 'gone native.' South America was his natural home ground. The stork all those years ago had dropped him in the wrong country. The small English town that he came from was the wrong destination.

'Curly' or 'Dennis the Dago' was small and wiry, had a hunched rolling gate nurtured by many a ship's deck, his splayed Chaplin-esque feet almost concealed shuffled beneath his over sized dungarees, nut browned by the sun, dark curly hair, drooping Zapata moustache and a hangdog look belied an intellect and wit within. Completing the chameleon transformation was his love and vast collection of exclusively grass-roots Latin, Central/South American records. Curly just loved his music, and could only have tolerated his comrades and their populist musical tastes, with their occasional comments like, 'What's that shit you playing Lampy?' whilst passing his cabin. That 'shit' would be a unique gem of a collection by today's discerning standards. He proudly banged those sounds out on his little record player, pleasuring himself like a man surrounded by eunuchs.

He often took off on his own when in port and would go missing into the hinterland whenever the opportunity arose, safely materializing the following day with the morning throng of the indigenous population looking years younger, a lovely life-affirming friendly bloke solitarily following his heart, whom I am sure by now sadly must be dead. I do wonder what might have become of his record collection.

The run ashore when in port was rarely that of a site-seeing tourist. More urgent intent was on making sure that time spent at sea deserved balancing up with blitzing whatever was on offer ashore. Bars, booze, bordellos, the potential for tricky moments and generally light-hearted bother increased with the evening's consumption, subject like all gatherings to the mellowness of all participating and the variety of venues sharing the load. Outcomes ranged from pure fun, albeit hazy and forgettable, getting back to the ship safely with a few escudos left in your pocket, to the strong possibility of staggering back in the small hours scuffed dishevelled and potless, feeling completely crap, and maybe worst, in just your underpants.

The legacy so far on this voyage was quite the norm, the odd case of crabs, one jump ship, who was returned at the next port of call, one fractured toe, a variety of sprained appendages, a black eye, and the inevitable incapacitating hangovers experienced by all at one time or another. There was interestingly a growing menagerie of livestock, including marmoset monkeys, a honey bear – an intriguing, small nocturnal creature somewhere between a koala bear and a squirrel – parrots, parakeets, and a jolly toucan. These live souvenirs often were bought when a little inebriated and weakened by beguiling onslaughts from a variety of vendors around the docksides. Whatever the circumstances were of the purchases it wasn't quite the practical thing to do. Conditions onboard were not conducive for caring and being responsible for squawking animals. But among seamen, out of necessity a tolerant lot, it was regarded as the norm.

So, there they were, in rickety cages dotted round the after deck, taking in the warm evening air. The wisdom of these purchases by some was slowly being questioned, especially when the weather became more inclement. The first to go were the marmoset monkeys. They were not ideal pet material and should have remained in the wild, but there was no discretion with the vendors, anything that moves sells. They were very small with devilish features and sharp little teeth and constantly screeched. It was well out of order, but their owner in a fit of despair lobbed them over the side. Then the parakeets' cage door somehow was left open, they were not seen again. There was one person who had cause to be disgruntled, he'd obtained a skinny drab green parrot, hunched and moulting, was told it was very young, and when grown would be a beautiful exotically coloured parrot. He was a mild mannered Able Seaman, lanky, slightly stooped, with sharp features and a prominent nose, uncannily just like his charge. He doted on his parrot, constantly talked to it and was convinced it was young as stated, it just looked a little rough due to its early neglect, and, with his loving tender care it would indeed emerge into a beautiful multi-lingual bird. Of course it was going down-hill by the day – owing to its age – but Lofty managed to pay off with bird still intact protectively carrying it ashore, and convinced with the notion, that 'once he got him home, he was sure that it would buck up.'

Most of the aforementioned menagerie was acquired in Guayaquil, Ecuador, our first port of call on the Pacific side of the South American continent, an area of the planet that did not quite exist some six hundred or so years ago, undiscovered and uncharted it would have been regarded as 'beyond the edge of the world' in the psyche of Europeans. Though it has been long mapped and colonised, to arrive there today by sea via Cape Horn or the Panama Canal, and on entering the Pacific, this blue exotic tropical paradise of an ocean, holds still a strange mysterious affect on the unconscious. The psyche of our forbears seems still to be laying dormant within, not yet completely evolved, subliminally affecting Europeans' behaviour, now that they are 'beyond the edge of the world', away from familiar waters and out of the confines of the staid controlling olde world. They seem to go a bit doolally, slightly more expansively than the first night in Benidorm madness, a brand new playground to misbehave in a carefree intoxication. 'Not guilty your honour! I was not myself! T'was the effect of falling over the edge!'

THE MANILLA ROPE

It was at this first port of call, tied up to the shanty-like dockside in a tributary servicing the city, that the first little bit of mania took place. Earlier in the day when the exotic bird and animal market was taking place, there was also activity going on in the other direction, at the opposite end of the ship, notably the observation by myself and another of the Chief Mate and Chief Steward furtively off-loading ship's stores to an equally looking furtive character who was bunging it into his banged up van. Maybe this was a little fiddle they had going each trip. We were in no doubt we had espied them 'bang to rights' selling ship's stores – 'our grub!' The perpetrators of this wheeling and dealing were the sometime arrogant virtuous sods with their braid and rule books who often in order to keep their aloof deference intact were unable to converse on an equal level. As result there was a subliminal shift in balance that may have affected our behaviour that evening.

The crew were ashore as soon as the working day had finished and a rapid shower taken. Mostly it was the deck hands, stewards and greasers who congregated around the seedier dives on offer. I can't recall the exact nature of the nightlife of Guayaquil – probably didn't get that far. Generally all these ports had areas that attracted seaman's pockets, at best a heady choice of venues with sometimes live indigenous music on offer with plenty of brass in the line up permeating the warm evocative evening air and so enlivening the perceived horizons of the innocents abroad who like moths to a light bulb bounced from bar to bar.

En-route back to the ship that evening we ended up in a dusty ramshackle bar frequented by day by dock workers – music supplied by a crackly radio – one last glug before staggering back on board. But, on this night, after more than one last glug

with some friendly locals accompanied with a passed around spliff (my first ever), a plan was hatched with our new friends. We agreed to sell them a mooring rope, the big bastard of a rope that ties the ship up, the spare one conveniently coiled up on deck ready to sliver over the side in the dead of night. Thanks to our boozy state and today's miscreants' activities fresh on our mind, it was an enthusiastic goer. We had conspired with total strangers to nick this sacred item of the ship – outrageous. Nothing less than keelhauling if caught.

All was well at the appointed hour when we crept up from our accommodation, onto the after deck and peered over the stern rail, beyond which the creek tapered off into the darkness. The air was still warm and the nighttime creatures were intermittently cricketing and croaking – we were three in number conspirators. On cue our new Ecuadorian mates emerged from the darkness in not what we were led to believe, a substantial boat to carry off what now looked increasingly a huge mountain of rope, but, paddling a canoe – biggish, but still a blooming canoe! We should have knocked it on the head then, but, they were keen, gesturing away for us to send the rope down. We had to assume they knew what they were doing with regards to big rope into little boat. So, we let them have it! In a few high octane moments we had the eye over and fed the rope down, they grabbed a hold and started to feed it into what seemed like an impossible space on the canoe. After that I could not look. We continued to feed it through and then it gained momentum and took off like a runaway train, and us not being in the steadiest of conditions jumped back absolving any further responsibilities of controlling the said rope as it was now doing a hundred miles an hour. At that very precise moment came loud shouts, not from the water as you might expect, but, from the deck amidships accompanied by wavy beams of torchlight heading aft at speed. The cadet officers were acting nightwatchmen – a must for these ports as there are some right thieving sods about. This was something in our inebriated euphoria we did not quite consider; alert watchmen.

Fortunately, although they'd noticed untoward activity going on we were not quite distinguishable, partially hidden by the after accommodation housing. As they came rushing down the port side of the deck we ducked around to the starboard side, knowing, lucky us, that was the entrance to our accommodation, just out of sight, into our cabins and in no time innocently tucked up in our bunks. Except, my cabin mate and co-conspirator failed to turn up. It emerged later he'd managed, whilst fleeing, to put his foot down a hawser opening in the deck and went flying and was lying there flat out when the cadets turned up, and immediately said on their arrival, 'The bastards, I nearly got 'em. They were only trying to nick the mooring rope!' He was believed wholeheartedly. He'd heard a commotion went up on deck and tackled the robbers, and was injured while bravely confronting them.

The aftermath fortunately was that of more evidence of the slippery nature of some of the locals, and the sterling work of a vigilant member of the crew. The rope snagged and was somehow retrieved. The half submerged canoe and its inhabitants managed to make it back into the darkness, but only after taking a few hits from objects that were at hand, lobbed at them with indignant enthusiasm by the cadets as if repelling the first Zulu charge.

MAN OVERBOARD

The ship was battened down going full ahead, two days journeying from Panama. It was late evening. Except for watch-keepers, the crew were all turned in, the night was black and moonless, and the sea had a slight swell with some mist. All seemed well, until, the usual clanking groaning propeller-churning noise of the seaman's accommodation was enlivened suddenly with shouts and much banging on doors.

'C'mon get up, get up on deck,'

'MAN OVERBOARD!'

The loose ensemble of deckhands yanked from their dreams mustered midships.

'What's happening?'

Amid much collective enquiry, the Bosun announces:

'We think Brummie has jumped over the side – he was last seen walking forward. The Mate wants us to form small groups and search the ship in case he's hiding somewhere. Alright chaps organise yourselves!'

The crowd although aware of the emergency of the situation, had trouble comprehending, how come Brummie's jumped, why? This is stupid. Further enlightenment came from the seaman who was on the watch at the time.

'It seems he's thrown some sort of wobbly, marched into the officer's accommodation and entered the old man's cabin, unannounced, woke him up muttering that he wanted to talk, yeah... wanted a chat. So the old man's bollocked him off and sent him to see the Third Mate, but, Brummie could not have wanted the Third Mate's first aid kit, so he never arrived. He was last seen strolling forward along the deck toward the foc'sle.'

Brummie was a Junior Ordinary Seaman, 17 years old, and harmless – which mattered little when small groups of grown men set out to search the nooks and crannies of the dark, dark, decks.

'What did the Mate mean, he may be hiding?' said one.

'Why should he be hiding?' said another.

And the inevitable retort, 'Cos he's got an axe and he's gonna jump out on us aaaaahhh!!!'

Big men spooked, scuttled off on a not very thorough search, and were quickly back to the warm glow of the mess room and safety in numbers.

The lookout had remained on the wing of the bridge. Normally lookout on that ship was kept on the monkey island exposed to the elements above the wheelhouse. Weeks at sea could go by without human contact with the inhabitants of the wheelhouse – the Deck Officers. From sundown to sunup watch-keeping lookout would trundle up and down the gangways and ladders in all weathers relieving their watch mates one hour on, one hour off. The only contact with the officer of the watch, in his warm dry environment, with hot drinks, sandwiches and in some cases gin, was to report by phone or bell the twinkling light that had just popped up on the horizon.

Tonight however was different, at least until we resumed our normal course. The wheelhouse door was open, the Mate was in and out, and a Cadet was on the wheel. A mug of tea proffered earlier by the Cadet cupped in the lookout's hands; some light conversation even takes place on the night's tragic events. Thoughts meandered through the lookout's mind, why? And why Brummie? Seventeen years old! Just too young, no warning, no prior wobblies, apart from maybe not seeming to be mixing with the crowd of late – not that unusual behaviour when banged up in a confined space, as occasional withdrawal helps with enduring the trip. He did after all miss the ship at the last but one port of call; again not that unusual, for after an over-indulgent run ashore the sailing deadline is missed. But now with hindsight this was a deliberate act by Brummie who just wanted to distance himself from the ship, desperate and ill-prepared he stood out in the small Peruvian port, was soon rounded up and delivered to the British Consulate representative and then transported to the next and final port of call, and there he rejoined the ship. Was duly logged and fined, in addition monies were extracted for the travelling and expenses incurred by the official.

It seemed almost an hour had passed by since the first flurry of activity when the ship had U-turned its four and a half thousand tons, chart positions plotted, helm orders given, not a quick and easy manoeuvre in the blind hope of going back onto its previous course to the spot where some poor soul had the madness to jump off. Some crew had sauntered back to their bunks, consensus, if taken, would surely have been 'he's had it!' And quite soon the order to resume course would be given, Board of Trade rules, human desire to search and rescue, optimism to keep looking against the odds all satisfied, after all, he did deliberately jump.

It was impossible to readily digest such a final act, to be so troubled, that went so unnoticed, that so surprised. The incredulity of one of your number taking leave in its purest violent form. On the one hand, suggesting all you close to me at this point in my life are to blame. Or, more kindly, why are you all carrying on when you know it's all a load of crap! I'm off! Cheerio. Not that simple or existential, more accumulative and invasive, which slowly burdens the fragility of your being until that moment arrives, when all the knocks, all the concerns, the all-pervading negativity gets a grip and takes over your actions. The reality of jumping without notice from the bow of a fast-moving ship, the height equivalent to roughly the roof of a terraced house, into the black abyss is a piece of piss in that certain state of mind.

However, to hit that cold wet nightmare and experience the complete shock to your senses is a pretty defining moment. Whatever took Brummie to this point I would like to think paled into insignificance immediately! Survival kicking in to endure the violent dunking, the buffeting, the pure horror of your situation as the huge hull of the ship pounds by you, your sanctuary is oblivious to your plight as it roughs you up in its wake, and, meanders further and further and further away, a twinkle of navigation lights receding slowly into the blackness. The consequences of that short sharp petulant act. So easy to do, so accessible, just hop over the rails. The rational you, that has kept you safe so far until this evening finally overwhelmed. How does it now contemplate the living nightmare, is it super conscious, are warm images of your life passing through your mind's eye, a clarity in slow motion, as so often related by people who have had brushes with near death? Or is there a self-preserving denial that tucks the feeling you, into a little compartment and proceeds to go on automatic pilot, like that of a sleepwalker? Or, purely, 'you stupid bastard, what did you do that for?' and further reprimand yourself as you slowly go under the surface without struggle because you are so pissed off with yourself and the finality of what you have done.

Whatever goes on, it is a horror situation, and a shudder goes down the spine if you imagine yourself in it, with the added hopelessness of the thought that no one had actually seen you jump at all.

Suddenly, unexpectedly, from out of the gloomy darkness there was a noise, a human sound, a sound not immediately discernible but enough to provoke a reminiscence of when laying in bed as a youngster and hearing the last garbled strands of a song, sung by a drunk wending his way home from the local pub.

No, this can't be. 'BRUMMIE!?' I shouted out loud, as I flew into the wheelhouse. Whether the Mate who went for the Aldis lamp – a large searchlight – was getting it for himself or me I don't know. I just grabbed it out of his hands and darted back out to the wing like my feet had never left the ground and aimed it into the darkness. The long beam of light penetrated ahead toward the drunken sounds. Nothing. Then, more audibly, a voice from the water clearly shouting. Somehow the shouts of '45°, 45°!' meant little to me as I was still frantically panning the darkness dead ahead. Then, a fleck of white catches my eye, nowhere near the eager beam of light, and, if not seen would have merrily drifted by, of course Brummie was shouting his position.

The light whacked onto Brummie and his lucky white tee shirt; centre stage. By then the ship, after a flurry of engine room signals and helm orders virtually came to a halt. Deck Hands were again summoned, the lifeboat got ready. A forever fixture on the ship's side inched away from its safe housing dripping with ropes and wires, swaying gently from the davits with its cargo still fresh from their bunks, it slowly descends and thuds onto the dark wet ocean. Engine actually starts, blocks away, chug, splutter, chug, splutter; the lifeboat vulnerably leaves its host behind and nudges slowly toward white tee shirt, fastened firmly by the ship's searchlight, finally drawing up to Brummie miraculously still treading water.

Eager arms reach out and catch hold. Brummie speaks.

'Fuck off, leave me alone!'

After 'Fuck off, leave me alone!', Brummie spoke no more. He was hauled into the lifeboat without a struggle.

*

A transcript from the official log book of the Cuzco;

Art. No. 16 A. Richards, JOS, Dis 'A' Book NO, R792337, came to my cabin at about 10.07pm and said he felt funny and could not sleep, though he appeared to me quite normal. I told him to go to the ship's dispensary and I would relieve the Third Officer [who was at the time on watch] so he could give him some tablets to help him sleep. Whilst explaining the situation to the Third Officer on the bridge, Richards again appeared a few minutes later and said he was looking for the Third Officer, I again instructed him to proceed to the dispensary and await the arrival of the Third Officer. The Third Officer then left the bridge and went down to the dispensary calling in at his room for the necessary keys, but on arrival and after a quick look around there was no sign of Richards.

Hands were alerted and a thorough search of the vessel made, but with no trace and it was then assumed the man had gone overboard. At 10.30pm the helm was put hard over to port and engine room warned of the situation and by 10.34pm the vessel was steaming on a reciprocal course of 172[g] the position was checked using RADAR and the course adjusted to 160[g] to make the position. At 10.39pm. Stand-by engine was rung and at 10.45pm, the position was again rectified and a course of 172[g] resumed. At 10.48pm, speed was reduced to half and at 10.51pm to dead slow when approaching the position. At 10.55pm the vessel stopped, at 10.59pm the lookout on the starboard wing of the bridge, Art. No. 13 M.J.Hugo EDH, reported hearing shouts from the water about two points on his bow. The Aldis was brought to bear on the position and the man spotted about 40/50 broad on the bow. Two life belts with light/smoke signals were released [the second brought over from the port wing of the bridge] and at 11.00pm engine put to full astern and at 11.01pm engine stopped. No.1 Motorboat was lowered and by 11.03pm was waterborne and at 11.05pm Richards was hauled inboard to the lifeboat. At 11.10pm Richards climbed out of the boat at the embarkation deck with remainder of the boat's crew and was taken to the ships hospital where he had a hot shower, a cup of tea with two 1.1/2 gram sedation tablets and was turned in. A constant watch was kept on him thereafter.

Arrangements will be made for this man to be landed in the Canal Zone as I do not feel justified in retaining him onboard for the Atlantic crossing to Rotterdam in his apparent mental state. 10.47pm, an auto alarm was sent followed by a message to all stations at 10.52pm, as follows: CUZCO/GKPF Lat 05.52 South Long 81.15 West MAN OVERBOARD 0312G.M.T. SEARCHING AREA BOUND BALBOA FROM SUPE VESSELS IN VICINITY KEEP SHARP LOOKOUT Signed MASTER. 11.13pm message cancelled, stating man had been recovered from the water At the time of the incident the ships course was 351.1/2[7]352[g] and the speed about 15.8 knots the wind was a gentle slight breeze with a slight sea and low swell, it was a moonless night, cloudy with a clear atmosphere.

Once back onboard he was minded constantly by the two cadet officers. The following afternoon he was seen being exercised on deck whilst handcuffed to both cadets, pretty much teenagers themselves, head slightly bowed and still saying nothing, a situation unimaginable a day or so earlier. Now a scene perfectly set as the trio promenaded along the deck, to mischievously imagine, if only there was a God of black comedy who felt like being amused, allowing Brummie to be afflicted with a surge of strength, usually associated with mad men and crack addicts, and still feeling the desperate urge to have another go then and there, despite – or forgetting – the handcuffs taking the two struggling cadets with him. Maybe the attempt ending with one cadet somehow jammed in the scuppers and the other one and Brummie connected by handcuffs dangling over the side.

The following day whilst still at sea I was approached while at work on deck by one of the mates, who informed me that Brummie had now spoken, and had specifically asked to speak to me!

'Blimey! Why me?'

'Don't know, just out of the blue insisted on speaking to you.'

'Oh well, ok'. Off we go to the cabin/hospital where he was under lock and key, and watchful eye.

'We'll have to lock you in with him, he doesn't want us present.' That's handy I thought.

It reminded me of a similar incident that took place on a previous ship that was also homeward bound from the South American continent, a meat boat laden with beef from Argentina. The Bosun, who was a huge gentle giant of a man with massive Popeye arms, had suddenly cracked up whilst talking to the Mate on deck about the coming day's work. He allegedly pointed out to the empty sea announcing to the Mate, look there is so and so, a former seaman who was also a jumper, and unrecovered, from a previous trip, and that he was sitting on a double-decker raft as large as life waving to the ship.

It would have been magical to have seen the Mate's expression change as it slowly dawned on him that the Bosun was not joking but deadly serious. How they dealt with him from that moment I am not sure, the talk was that he had been straightjacketed at some point, not that he was being threatening, just precaution. He was powerfully built, no doubt sedated then released, but, kept under lock and key in one of the deck cabins under twenty four hour watch by the deck watch-keepers, one hour on – one hour off, the person relieving would hold the key, unlock the door, let his watch mate out, enter and be locked in by his mate, banged up with this hulk of a deranged bloke for a whole hour. This went on until we reached the nearest port, which happened to be Rio, fortunately a day or so away. If it had happened after, that we would have been deep sea, so it was just for one nighttime watch that I had the pleasure of keeping the Bosun company.

His Gulliver-like body laid out, sedated to the bunk. There was one hairy moment when he suddenly awoke and was looking troubled and agitated and seemed scared as if something was about to happen. Oh no! I had still a half hour to go before being relieved. He was becoming more agitated and looking around. He noticed me sitting on a chair in the corner of the cabin trying to dematerialise.

'Bose, Bose, you alright?' Forced into making my presence known in as friendly manner as possible.

'It's me, Mick... everything's ok... what? What's up?' Leaning forward, connecting more visibly.

'Bose, you've just been a bit unwell.' Noticing that he hasn't made a move to attack me, I realise he's mouthing words.

'Who's trying to get you?'

'Little men! ... Little Dagoes, with gas guns trying to gas me!'

'No, you're all right Bose. No one's trying to get you.'

'They are! They are! They're coming out of the vents, they're gonna gas me!'

Like a nightmare that doesn't dissipate on awakening, he seriously was disturbed by this apparition, and me too. 'Dagoes coming out of the air-conditioning vents!' Next minute I'm up on my feet to defend my Bosun. Rushing up to the air vent situated on the bulkhead and fending off the Dago attack using all the expletives and war cries I could summon from my comic reading days, and then pounding the vent triumphantly.

'Gurron yer Dago bastards!'

Seemingly to the satisfaction of the Bosun who slowly settled back down. no longer under threat, with a faint whisper of a smile he went back to sleep.

So, into the cabin I step, key turns the lock on the door behind me.

'Alright Alex!' Brummie's name said in that upbeat cheery matey manner. One never knows. Brummie spoke at length, in a friendly and wholly confessional manner, about his early childhood, of his disruptive and drama-filled home life as a result of his alcoholic parents, of being farmed out with his sister to Ireland into the care of his granny, a blissfully calm and happy period, and then emotively to be brought back to the Midlands to the bosom of his temporarily reformed parents, only to soon experience once more the alcohol-fuelled violence and abuse whilst again trapped in the family home.

The impulse to run off to sea at fifteen would have been a mighty draw. His telling me of other woes, and his inability to sleep securely, included significantly an incident whilst asleep in his bunk on a previous ship, when he was attacked by a drunken Bosun with a spike who'd entered his cabin, out of his head on drink – the very man who should, like the Captain of the present ship, be a father figure, protective towards the younger seamen under his care. When Brummie went to the Captain, breaching that bullshit divide, he was desperate – the outraged response to the intrusion was a bollocking, with no one else to turn to he wandered off into the darkness and took his leave.

There were also the inevitable recent incidents and the odd fracas that took place along that mad coast, generally to be expected as the occurrence of turbulent seas given the climate of the workplace. Brummie's space had no doubt been encroached upon and had become untenable, sufficient for him to jump ship in a small far off Peruvian port. Not exactly a comfort zone.

Brummie was naturally deemed unfit to continue the voyage and was put ashore in Panama into the care of the British Consul and temporarily hospitalised, and then to have been flown back to the UK, presumably to receive some sort of psychiatric counselling and no doubt an end of a career at sea. Not so; I discovered some time later, he was back to sea within six months.

En route home, the ship was sold and diverted to Rotterdam where the new moody owners or maybe even the current, ran up the Panamanian flag. We had a night in Rotterdam where I picked up a farewell logging and finally paid off. Further transport home was courtesy of a coach trip to Dunkirk then ferry to Dover, no doubt the least expensive route. I don't recollect sharing the journey with uniformed members of the crew. Being summertime the ferry was heaving with returning holiday makers, by the time that we had got there and boarded some drink had already been consumed, so it was straight to the bar in which we were domiciled thereafter for the whole crossing.

The remaining remnants of the menagerie in their cages were discreetly secreted under the tables. The honey bear that had been asleep in its box, being nocturnal, had been placed into an empty cabin. The ferry departed, there was a respectful integration by all in the bar amid a somewhat party atmosphere, darkness fell and the preoccupation of drinking and chatting lead to a relaxing of duties of care.

Suddenly there were screams and children running. The honey bear had awoken and managed to get out of his box. There was slight pandemonium until it was retrieved and brought into the bar, panic soon turned to interest by the passengers and the cute honey bear was soon jumping from table to table enjoying the attention. This however in the growing relaxed atmosphere prompted a response from others who were soon proudly displaying their beloved pets. The toucan a lovable gentle creature took up residence on the bar hopping up and down and one parrot managed to spread its wings to the glee of all the patrons.

When we arrived at customs we were all by now well pissed and the seen-it-all-before customs officers obviously felt it was not worth their while to even pretend to process us, ushered us and animals straight through. For some reason I'd obsessed about a watch that I'd bought in Rotterdam and wanted to declare it for some reason or other – something about future travel – and was being insistent brandishing the watch attached firmly on my wrist at times millimetres from the customs man's nose due to heavily swaying in a jerky circular fashion and was told by Mister Customs Officer.

'Look mate, I'm not telling you again. Fuck off through will you!'

BOSUNS

You could safely say that at any one given moment in time, there would be the likelihood of finding a Stornawegian on a British merchant vessel. How a minute island like Stornaway, one of the few larger islands on the west coast of Scotland, produces so many seafarers, I don't know. It would strike any one's mind to idly imagine that the milkmen and postmen of that fair isle, in good old music hall – nudge-nudge, wink-wink – mode, had a rare old time with all the men-folk being at sea.

The Stornawegians that I'd met had a great capacity for drink, aside from the rare evangelical total abstainer – there was no middle ground. I wasn't exactly sheltered from Gaelic accents in my cockney preserve. Among friends were first generation Irish or Scots with broad accents that were not much of a problem, but I just could not understand the Stornaway tongue, which was further complicated by a high-pitched delivery. They were certainly different, like inhabitants from a small as yet undiscovered island sort of way, likeable yet weird, a race apart, totally dedicated to work and drink, with a capacity to hold it and remain unchanged as if it were like the intake of food, a necessity for sustenance learnt at an early age, culturally indelible, reinforced by observing their elders.

I sailed a couple of times under Stornawegian Bosuns, both likeable and undemanding with no complexities, just an effort to understand. I'm convinced that shipping companies, given the choice, would much prefer the hardy fellows of Stornaway to wholly man their ships than a motley crew from the rest of the British Isles. One was memorable for being known as 'The Hollywood Bosun'. One could think, ah, maybe at some point in the past he had been involved in a film, or maybe when he had shipped out to the U.S. he found himself in a dockside crowd scene of the movie On The Waterfront – 'Whoa! Marlon Brando, he deserves the nickname!'

No, I gathered purely that it was because he had a mild baby face look, not as rough as his compatriots and a head of blond hair that he permanently coiffured like the old Teddy Boy's quiff. These two features constituted Hollywood status among his sea-going Stornaway peers. What celebrity! What glamour! As he toddled off the island ferry onto the wind-swept dock of Stornaway on a rare visit home, as the gnarled old ferry skipper looked on from his bridge mouthing in his wake, 'There ye go, ye fecking poove' ye!' Not a fan of fancy hair-do's!

Bosuns were recruited from the more experienced of the Able Seaman, them that have a good record of behaviour and a sense of responsibility. For their elevation they were required to tread the fine line between what would have been their crewmates, but with one foot in the Officer camp, becoming, along with the Lamp-Trimmer, carpenter, and electricians, a Petty Officer. The Bosun was the foreman of the deck crew, putting them to work and turning them out for stations, he liased with the Chief Mate with regard to work programmes. He also needn't, apart from admin, actually do any work, he kept clean. Just a few of them because of this slight detachment stick out in memory.

On an early ship there was a hard-boiled Bosun who could be summed up by one major incident in his life. As a one-company man his incident became a part of company lore and well-known to all. He had somehow got his leg entangled in a topping lift wire that hauled him aloft upside down at a great speed presumably because a heavy raised derrick that the wire was attached to had unsecured and hurtled down to the deck. The Bosun's foot was disengaged from his leg when the wire whizzed through the topping lift block, immediately sending the foot-loose Bosun from a fair height back down to the deck. It was whilst the Bosun was in mid-air he managed, before he hit the deck, to not, as might have been expected from his sudden predicament, let out a shrill spine-tingling scream that would be indelibly printed on the minds of all present for the rest of their lives – instead shouted out 'UNDER BELOW!!!' A phrase used as general rule if something was dropped from aloft when working to warn those working below, whose response would be hands on head and take off like a rabbit.

This warning was very admirable given in possibly the last split second of his existence. No need for holding heads and running off like rabbits – those working alongside him witnessed the Superman take-off thinking maybe, 'What's he playing at?' and then just open-mouthed dumbstruck awe as he back-flipped back to earth minus a foot. He managed to miss all below including winches and various lethal bits of deck paraphernalia and miraculously survived the fall, albeit somewhat badly injured though conscious. In the pandemonium of the aftermath a spooked member of the crew picked up the grizzly appendage, still in its shoe, and threw it over the side – as if it were some evil being. The conscious Bosun observed this act and screamed out 'You bastard!', in the direction of the seaman who threw the severed foot, 'I JUST BOUGHT THEM FUCKING SHOES!!'

Affectionately known as Popeye, an old Able Seaman and ex-Bosun, frail and not quite up to physical demands, was now seeing out his twilight years as Bridge Quartermaster, a token easy number courtesy of his long company standing. He should have been in restful retirement if he had ever had a home or a semblance of shore life. Endearingly he still mucked in with the lads when grog was being passed around.

We were in Lisbon, shore leave now suspended and expecting to sail soon, but drinking continued. The cramped cabin full of the urgent needy, the ones who had been ashore that day and were half pissed and bent on continuation. On what was a largeish ship it was unlikely that the same gathering would again be repeated, for one or two it might have been an occasional trip blowout, others may be on duty or in another 'soirée' in another cramped cabin when afflicted with the drink; like the inhabitants of a train carriage, never to be replicated. Popeye was unique. He had survived the war years as one of the most vulnerable, a 'merchant seaman'. He had been bombed, torpedoed, spent days in lifeboats, shipwrecked and castaway on an isolated coastline in West Africa for many weeks, and still willingly continued with a life on the sea. His outlook was refreshingly unencumbered by the same old bollocks of a lifetime of these gatherings.

There were these goatskin leather teat-like bags of Spanish origin called botas containing crap wine being passed around. The idea was to hold up the bag at a short distance from your face, aim the teat toward your open mouth and squeeze, a modicum of skill necessary to successfully aim it toward your mouth and nowhere else.

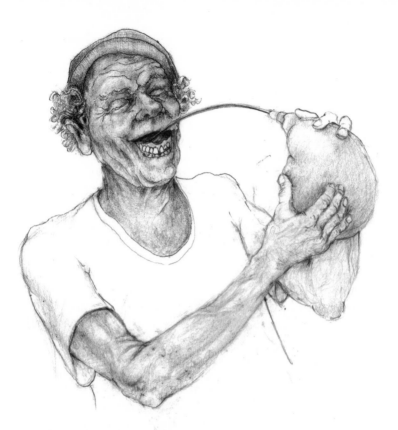

I was sitting next to Popeye in this pathetically cramped shebeen, relishing this ancient mariner in a pissed insightful way that normally you would have taken for granted (just some old bastard on board), when it was his turn to grasp the leather wine bag. Now in his hands he nursed it lovingly, unhurried and poised. He then announced as if making a short speech in homage to the impending glug that he was about to take from the collective bag of wine.

'Sod today! Forget yesterday! And bollocks to tomorrow!' A short cheer emanated from the merry drinkers. He then with great deliberation and decorum raised the leather pouch, opened his mouth and squeezed, an arc of wine aimed perfectly, entered, his eyes closed in ecstasy. Suddenly, his upper false teeth fell and clattered shut against his lower teeth, whether it was well practised cool or just blissful oblivion his mouth remained open as he continued to receive the arc of wine now entering his mouth between his gums and upper teeth. With a cool display of purpose and a fixed surreal toothy grin anatomically misplaced now hurdled comfortably by the stream of wine, he completed his intake without mishap closed his mouth re-engaging his teeth, then with a gnarled forefinger placed under a hang-dog blood shot eye, uttered slowly as if an afterthought, too old now with a life time of consequences to be flippant.

'But!... Be sure... to keep a wary eye open!'

By the time the wine went round again, Popeye was blissfully snoring mouth open, his upper teeth perilously hanging on.

Sometimes the aftermath of these boozy occasions promoted puerile activity, and often the victims, laid low by the intake of drink, became the recipients. If they had managed to take to their bunk a favourite was to sew up the bottom of the opening to one of the legs of the work trousers laid strewn on the floor – or both if you could be bothered. The ensuing struggle, though not witnessed when they finally roused from their stupor, late for watch or stations, and are inevitably in a high state of confusion, is relished when the sewing task is successfully completed and the perpetrators giggle their way back to their bunks. Other items of clothing can also be sewn, a heavy metal deck shackle sewn into a pocket promotes a 'what the fuck!?' moment, along with shoes impossibly knotted together by the shoelaces, sheets turned back before victims turn in, can produce confused frantic kicking, resulting in a crunched up foetal position for the rest of the night because they are too zonked to do anything about it.

Light-hearted petty prank feuds sometimes developed and reached a crescendo when one or other party went over the top, like when a good mate of mine – no one was sacred – a steward, had crashed out. I crept into his darkened cabin to give him the boot polish treatment and guided by his staccato snoring in my haste instead of tagging him with a light covering of polish, I managed to stuff a wodge of it into his mouth; he was off sick for a week. I shamefully owned up though he knew I was the likely perpetrator. Pranks did get a bit out of hand at the time including in the dead of night cabin doors being thrown open and buckets of iced water lobbed over the sleeping inmates. An uneasy truce prevailed as result of my dangerous botched boot polish job and people took to locking their doors.

When signing on Ship's Articles, at the beginning of a trip there is provision made for sending home an allotment, a proportion of your wages at regular intervals to family or next of kin. This would be a necessity for crew with dependants. There were no regular payments of wages made whilst at sea. A main payment of your balance would be made on completion of the trip, 'pay-off day.' In the meantime, during the many months at sea, if you needed cash when in port you were required to ask for a 'sub'. The limit available was always less than you would have liked and bearing no relation to the ample credit that you may have with wages earned to date. After a cap in hand queue outside the purser or mate's cabin you inevitably found the amount of pocket money received had been decided for you. Like a parent to a child to prevent them from spending too much money in the sweet shop.

The bond however would be open when at sea at selected times for cigarettes, tobacco, and beer, signed for and deducted on the day of reckoning. A tax-free carton of two hundred cigarettes cost ten shillings (50p). As was general almost all did smoke. In fact the term 'tea break' was never uttered unless you were a complete rookie and it would just be the once. It was known as 'smoko', a most welcome sound when suffering on deck in angry weather. 'SMOKO' as nice to relay the message as it was to hear it.

Basic toiletry bits were also obtained from the bond. Bedding such as fresh sheets and pillow cases were provided once a week, which makes me feel shameful when compared to my now once a quarter. Cabins – the quality of varied from ship to ship and the age that it was built and the pecking order of the occupants. As a Deck Boy I was in a four-berth. Commonly the norm was two-berth for ratings, only a few shipping companies that were not retarded provided single-berth cabins for all the crew.

The defining of a character and all its manifestations is mostly observed and experienced within family life. The close proximity of siblings and parents set the stage, the larger the family the more the variety, but it does increase the likelihood of long-term casualties. The whole gamut of emotional evolution leading to an individual adult character is laid bare. Then, it is goodbye! The umbilical cord that connects you to your 'lovely family' is there for you to stretch, break, or rope in! According to your take on the family experience, then off into the world to be finely or roughly honed, and then tweaked according to circumstances, consciously and unconsciously.

The responsibility is yours and how you felt so far about yourself to choose for the moment a hypothetical destination that at least gets you out of the door. To then select, be selected, get dragged along, mysteriously happen upon, wake up with, or not move an inch. The outcome is subject very much in flavour rather than type to economic and class position as to partner, friends and social grouping. Not unlike the production run of a theatre, when the audience and players are in confinement during the performance, a ship on its voyage provides a metaphorical stage for cameo roles for all onboard, some of these finished articles provoked the same wide eyed response as a first night at the theatre.

Once at sea, initial prejudice and early judgement of people oh so slowly overturns when in an enforced collective exile, and far from home. Patient humanity wins through when there is nowhere to hide and constant exposure. Arseholes become likeable, nutters become friends, and snobby bastards become equals. Not wanting to get too carried away with this evangelical enlightened observation. You still on occasion may want to see a certain individual topple over head first into an empty hatch. But it passes. The heartening feeling from being at sea was how well everyone got on. This however would obviously not extend in the event of a shipwreck, when survivors make it to uninhabited foodless island and the weakest among them is being eyed up by the rest with thoughts of barbecued buttock.

Let us hope civilisation doesn't wholly crack. Us; the objective animal, blessed with consciousness that has slowly refined our innate primate within, reinforced throughout time by dramatic interventions with etched tablets, reams of text, and utterances from seers and prophets and the finest of our ancestors' minds as to the do's and don'ts of how we should all behave. So that we may carry on sitting round campfires singing hearty songs about love and dreams, and, I suppose still, if survival dictates, be eating permissible amounts of skewered buttock.

On the subject of hunger, food onboard was always a bit of an issue, especially early on when, freshly-divorced from home cooking, and slowly improving from surviving on toast, to drinking tea and almost enjoying it with disgusting condensed milk. There were good feeders and bad feeders, good feeders were more of a rarity and subject to the individual passion and creativity of the ship's cooks, who managed to uplift the amount and quality of the stores at their disposal. The bad feeders, with their uninterested galleys, varied in their badness as is usual in captive institutions, along with the acceptance of company penny-pinching and grubby hands creaming prior to sailing. It is hard to imagine during the food chain anyone agonising about the menu and standard of produce that entered the seaman's stomach, only maybe, a consideration for an apartheid preference to the officer class who ate their tweaked meals with a silver service and attendant stewards. What's new? All were fed, no reports of scurvy and no live weevils to be found in mouldy biscuits. If you were to be historic about it, today's seaman had never had it so good, one's culinary lot was in the hands of fate. It was hardly expected to have expectations once you had pushed off to sea.

Respite was occasional, when ashore, with the delights of local indigenous food on offer, if desirous and time was found in between refreshments, which wasn't often. But there were times like when tied up for the week at the docks in La Plata, Argentina, meals would rarely be eaten on board. Instead the shacks on the dockside that primarily serviced the dockers who loaded the prime beef would be sought out by the ship's crew and frequented daily. Often to be found would be some burly unshaven sweaty hombre amid the smoking grills and hotplates plying seamlessly the trade of cooking the biggest most succulent steaks you had ever seen. Lumps of flesh were deftly flipped with a large spatula that also swatted the odd bothersome fly that came into view. Then with juices flowing, flopped into half of a loaf of the tastiest bread and accompanied with a carafe of cheapo that happened to, under the circumstances, feel like fittingly sublime wine. There was of course fine dining to be had and cheaply in the restaurants of the Corrientes, but street food as found in most parts of the world, if brave enough to partake sometimes into the unknown, always hit the spot.

Not to be confused with the contents of the hot meat pies on offer at the dockside cafe at Custom House. Doused with lashings of HP sauce and accompanied with a mug of Camp coffee – the liquid chicory stuff – a first introduction to foreign seamen, if they're brave enough, of British working man's cuisine.

If you took to the world of being on the sea, then without fail an intoxicated love of ships would befall you. Maybe not so much today's modern container ships, tankers, bulk carriers, the streamlined hi-tec colossus beasts of the sea providing wonderful conditions for seamen. But, like so many areas of life now they are so far from the aesthetically pleasing, people-friendly managed environments that were – square rigger days aside – still embodied in the engine-powered ships of yesteryear. These slowly faded out at the onset of containerisation and automation, dispensing bodies forever redundant and contributing to the demise of the British merchant fleet.

When joining a ship and making your way through the bustle of the dockside to your workplace and home for the duration of the impending voyage, it felt exclusive and somehow secret as it would soon slip its moorings, sometimes in the dead of night when tides dictate and London slept, carrying you down river thence off to distant shores. Clambering aboard one of these ships up the swaying gangway clasping the rope handrail, its nature unchanged since the invention of the wheel, the natural fibres connecting as one with the same hand as our ancestors, a dominant remnant of our sailing ship days still ever present. The same for the huge beautifully plaited manila mooring ropes so malleable and grip friendly for something so big and strong that rigidly holds fast the huge tonnage-laden ships. There is an emphatic complete confidence in the woven fibres of a rope no matter what size by those who have had the privilege in their working or leisure activities to have handled the beautiful stuff.

Once on board you had stepped onto and into another world, a hybrid attachment inhabited by representatives of every colloquial nuance of the British Isles, banged up 24/7 with dodgy accents, quirky characters and unfamiliar reference points, with whom you would have to eat, drink, share cabins, socialise, and work. This eclectic mob soon became your adopted family. The combined sounds, odours and movements of the ship also soon become familiar and comforting, the odd whiff of oil, hemp, tallow, canvas, red lead, galley smells, the sea breeze the changing seas, the creaking, heaving, sunrise, sunset, engine churning, screws turning, bells ringing and all the while night and day logging sea miles, while negotiating the elements along plotted courses to finally arrive at otherwise unattainable destinations for its inhabitants, if, the choice they made when pondering, was not to have gone to sea.

Everyone onboard has a status and laid down duties to perform, and once this hybrid detaches from its mother and sails off to foreign parts, under the surface of its civilian enterprise will be a microcosm of the English class system and accompanied rules to maintain law and order, which was thankfully nothing like the law and order or the regimented discipline of the Royal Navy. As long as you turned out to do the work that was expected of you and covered your back it was a perfectly carefree life. But, there was division. I am sure that many deck officers and sea captains have come through the ranks having working-class origins, 'Well done chaps!' But this was not a naturally encouraged route. Unlike climbing the ladder in numerous shore-based industries, it smacked of bullshit, control and pomp. Though it probably rates quite low in the occupations inhabited by the ruling classes, it still attracts a proportion of the dumbos of their litter into fundamentally a middle-class 'officer and gentleman' regime that one would be naïve to expect any change. A stint in the Australian Merchant Navy was completely refreshing, and a perfect example of equality and functioning without the need for bullshit. Anyways, everyone was in it together and whatever your denomination, the experience of being on a ship and going off to sea was yours and yours alone.

For the deck crew outward bound on a lengthy trip, generally one of the main tasks would be overhauling the ship's gear. This was pleasant work, which felt useful and required basic deck work seamanship, such as rope splicing or going aloft in bosun's chairs. Great fun when compared with the usual tasks, homeward bound, which amounted to the monotony of banging away all day with chipping hammers relieving the decks of layers of old paint and repainting the whole ship, apart from of course the ship's sides, which, often were tackled where possible when anchored or tied up in port. Painting the ship's side was also fun as this was undertaken from stages thrown over the side and secured by ropes. Probably a more precarious system than the bosun's chair. Because it took two of you to handle each end of a plank of wood, a smaller sized length of timber was attached, overlapping the sides of the plank referred to as 'horns' where the ropes at both ends were secured, equally suspending the stage horizontally, then up through a block tied to the ship's rail then back down and lashed to the plank. This pulling part of the rope was used to lower and raise the stage. The knots and hitches for this exercise were very specific and if not done right could be a tad catastrophic – which was why painting the ship's side was potential fun as you would of course be dangling in the air with the water a fair way below. There would be pots of paint and roller trays also lashed on to the plank. The monitoring of work when in port was always a bit lax, with attention diverted by the business of unloading and loading of cargo, and with the ship having recently arrived after a while at sea, everyone was likely to be experiencing the morning after the night before, which could drag on for a few days if it were a good port. The consequence was the inevitable dunking or someone ending up paint-splattered and holding on for dear life to the end of a now vertical painting stage. This would occur as a result in equal measures of ineptness, unsteady reactions and sabotage.

If it were a longish passage, work would settle down to a relaxing pattern of day work, watch keeping and sobriety. No tv, no radio, no newspapers, regular meal times, sufficient sleep, bracing sea air and predominantly tropical weather with constantly changing astronomical night skies, no family responsibilities, no bills to pay, no what to wear worries, no need for money in the pocket... Aye, 'twas hard!

The best watch to be on for aesthetics and economics was the 4 – 8 watch. On lookout there is the glory of the sun rising and the sun setting, supreme in a 360° horizon and there is the opportunity to work six hours overtime to top up the pretty poor wages and still manage meal times and a decent sleep. Fairness did prevail and watches did rotate.

THE FREAK WAVE

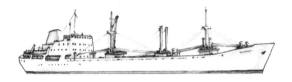

It however was not all bliss – inclement weather and changing conditions were always hovering unseen and waiting to pounce just beyond the horizon. The following are two absolute bottle going incidents that I encountered, one whilst on the Beaver Ash, a Canadian Pacific Line ship part of a group of 'Beaver' boats plying between Britain and Canada. It was winter time in the North Atlantic, the ship, on its way to St Lawrence, Canada, received new orders to proceed to St John, New Brunswick, owing to the Saint Lawrence river being frozen over, an annual occurrence.

It was the coldest I'd ever felt. The icy conditions during the latter stage of the crossing meant no one ventured on deck. The seas were tumultuous with huge swells and deep troughs, the ship seeming more and more insignificant as it surfed like a spectacular 'Sea World' roller coaster ride. It really livened up being on the wheel, and the buzz at being privy to steering this master ride. Finally, able to go up on deck on approaching arrival at St John it was like stepping into an alien landscape; the ship petrified and disfigured by packed ice. We were given the job of freeing up some of the necessary apparatus for docking, and this meant pathetically bashing away at the ice with whatever implements we could muster, making hardly an impression before feeling that your fingers were about to drop. My frozen digits were encased within two pairs of gloves plus a woolly pair of socks on top. Not much time was spent on that activity.

We finally docked and tied up, and once snuggly in port and out of the driving winds, it felt positively warm. I did feel that cold in that part of the world drier and more bearable than that of the British wet variety. Little did we know that this episode of harsh weather would not be our last.

St John lays in what is now the Province of New Brunswick. Historically an area central to the battles for occupation by the colonising French and English that raged for many generations. Its prized natural wealth and land-grabbing attainment resulted in multiple suffering by all concerned and the death knell of the indigenous North American Indian. Now its sanitised, pioneering image with a backwoods history of nature providing permeates modern day living.

A strong memory I have was that of the foreman of the gang of dockers unloading the ship. Who, probably as a sign of status, theatrically strode around dishing out orders in a full length bearskin fur overcoat and a matching Davy Crocket-styled fur hat. I found it hard to imagine his counterpart in London docks in a similar attire.

We were a couple of days out, and homeward bound, when the weather started to roughen up. I was off watch and trying to sleep in my cabin, with some difficulty, as the ship was violently pitching and rolling. Suddenly an almighty bang virtually threw me out of my bunk. Something had smashed into the port side of the ship. I was dressed in a flash and opened the cabin door, and there before my eyes was ankle-deep water running along the passageway. I am positive if that was me now in that situation I would have thought the end was nigh, instead of my remembered bemused inquisitive reaction – Mmm, this looks fun!

We had been hit by a 'Freak Wave', an unexpected phenomenon, a calling card reminding you of nature's awesome power. Throughout time this has been the prime candidate responsible for all the mysterious disappearances of shipping in the open seas; a solitary wave slowly building strength and height along the vast oceans creeping up on unsuspecting victims then, wallop! Devouring all within its path, a tsunami triggered by certain conditions as opposed to an earthquake.

The ship, a reasonably small cargo vessel of 2,300 tons, had two lifeboats just sufficient for all crew, one on each side of the ship. The result of that one almighty impact was the port lifeboat disappeared completely. The davits where it was safely housed were left mangled and twisted. Also gone was the ten-ton gangway box, once securely bolted to the deck, handrails and railings either taken away or left in an abstracted condition. A large capstan on the after deck was taken on a visit to the ocean floor, and the whole port side left in a general battered state.

The engine room had taken water, either through vents or the funnel, indicating the vast height of the wave; fortunately not disabling any machinery that may have effected the ship's power or manoeuvrability; a nightmare scenario. We immediately 'hove to', meaning altering course to go in the direction of or against the waves. This was a safer option than the constant battering if we remained side on to the weather. This possibly should have taken place earlier on, in consideration of ship safety. Of cause going totally off course is a somewhat desperate decision to make and not commercially viable.

The water that alarmingly penetrated the inner sanctum symbolically elicited the worst fears for all seafarers. That 'sinking feeling' was just the residue of the mountain of water that took the capstan away and entered the void it left, pouring into the after steering gear room below and the adjacent crew accommodation. Sailing ships of yesteryear would have had no chance whatsoever.

It was interesting when finally entering the London docks. Dockers and dock officials were all gawping up at the battered ship's side. It felt like we were heroically limping into port having suvived a wartime battle.

THE HURRICANE

My second humbling experience was in the tail end of one of the inappropriately, predominantly female named, hurricanes that rear up annually in the Caribbean. The personalising is a bit disarming, affectionate even, and who I have wondered, gives them their names? Do they reference The Book of Baby Hurricane Names?

We were deep into the night, and I was on lookout duties up on the open area of the monkey island, where the big binnacle was housed, just above the wheelhouse, maintaining Board of Trade requirements to have lookout at all times. Although on this evening it was impossible. The conditions of zero visibility and the worst weather imaginable, lookout should have been brought into the warm, dry confines of the wheelhouse and vigilance left to the all-seeing radar. This hadn't occurred to the officer below, or that the poor fellow outside may be suffering. So dutifully I adhered to the code of not leaving one's station until relieved by my fellow or following watch mate. The suffering that I allude to was that although I was aware that ships, like planes, have lightning conductors for protection, it gave very little assurance when all around you a bombardment of bolts of lightning were striking into the sea interspersed with sheet lightning lighting up the sheer fragility of the tons of wet iron and steel that you were perched on, cowering, sodden by the driving rain that almost hurt, ears boxed by frightening loud thunder claps waiting for any minute to be turned to cinder by a direct hit.

My bottle by now was completely gone. Ten minutes before my relief arrived I deserted my post and skinned out for what I thought was for my life. I battled my way down the companionway, fearful now of being uplifted like a piece of insignificant litter and blown over the side. Finally I'm into the sanctuary of the mess-room, frazzled having been an audience of one to an almighty fearsome show.

My watch mate was sitting rigid, hands clasped round a mug of tea muttering, 'Fuck that! I'm not going up there.'

There were also other strange phenomena that occurred, that must have freaked out those burgeoning ancient mariners when the earth was deemed flat. Two that I had experienced included an electrical storm that lit up the ship's mast, known as 'St Elmo's Fire'. You can just imagine these sailors, fearful of the almighty, falling to their knees when viewing their mast and spars seeming to be ablaze with fire. The other more gentle and aesthetic took place in the Sargasso Sea, near the Azores. Seemingly inexplicably, the whole area of sea around the ship during the hours of darkness was alight with a bright fluorescent green shimmering mysteriously. The ship gently slicing through, producing glittering Tinkerbell dust bough waves. This apparition was due to a certain type of plankton massing and floating just below the surface.

Homeward bound was a recuperative period; the toll of mad jaunts finally cleansed by the time of arrival in British waters and finally tying up in London docks, voyage completed. Bright as bunnies back home after numerous weeks spent sailing to a variety of destinations, events that had taken place under exotic and not so exotic backdrops now behind and confined to memory. The day of severing links with ship and company and the signing off of articles, a most anticipated day after exhausting the joys and tribulations of new horizons. Pay-off day. The day to pick up what always

seemed a comparatively meagre amount of money left of your earnings for your efforts and incarceration for indeterminate periods. Ultimately though it did not matter. To get home in the tail end of the British winter having just spent time in hot climes felt good. It wasn't usual to see people with tans outside of summer at that time. Package holidays did not quite exist for all, so, it was somewhat glamorous to turn up after months of absence, sun blushed, be-suited, a few quid in the bin, and a line of slightly embellished stories of foreign travels involving a variety of docksides. At least, it was like that for a day or two, then, absorption into shore life, and I was once again kicking my heels with my mates.

Easily I would slip back into the fold, taking my place among the huddle on the corner – as in a soap opera, you can miss numerous episodes and not fundamentally miss a thing. The characters remain the same, and if anything eventful had taken place the bunnying on, and retelling of events – especially if the outcome was favourable and included some poor sod's demise – soon filled in the gaps during the coming days spent in cafes and hanging out on the corner.

THE SEAMENS STRIKE

To some extent to be exposed to the big wide world of different people and different cultures, at such a young age and with otherwise no prospects, was a unique privilege. But, it set a precedent for a proneness to being footloose and the development of a strong aversion to a sedentary life style. If there were apprenticeships and situations to be had by starting as a boy to obtain skilled attributes or worthwhile trades the possibility of being eligible receded with every year spent at sea.

Generally the longer that you stayed at sea the harder it was to integrate back into shore life. Ultimately marriage and begetting would/could force the issue for some, but, to take the initiative – with seamanship skills not translating into shore work – meant presenting yourself for whatever factory-type menial jobs were on offer.

Static situations vacant, that left you feeling vacant and as lost and helpless as a beached whale. I once in a moment of desperation responded to a big recruitment drive by the Ford motor plant at Dagenham for workers. They were literally taking on anybody. At the interview after a glance at my seaman's book – my CV – I was told, 'Sorry mate! You wouldn't last the day!' Though miffed at rejection, they were dead right.

However, even though the carefree unencumbered outsider lifestyle of a seafarer was a major attraction, it does after a time become as repetitious as the Ford conveyor belt. Coupled with the feeling that you are not putting down civilized roots, and fearing that the longer you leave your departure the more likely you will have disabled your ability somewhat to communicate – already feeling like a visiting tourist when on home leave – slowly becoming more unsure by not sharing everyday aspirations.

My time for leaving was chosen for me by the national seamen's strike of 1966. I was home on leave at the time and

eagerly participated in the protest activities. For my picket duties
I was assigned to the dock gates of a small basin in Thomas
More Street, across from St Katharine's Dock (Tower Bridge).
I think there were a couple of barges in there at the time, but, I
manfully stood my ground ready to ward off 'scabs', then as
soon as it was decent I'd jump the 67 bus and was home within
fifteen minutes.

My union office was in Red Lion Street, just off of Cable
Street, where we congregated for duties and on Friday our
strike pay – £3 per week, which went up to a whole £5 one
week when the television cameras were there, then back down
to £3 when they had gone.

The strike had been called by the National Union of Seamen
over pay and conditions. I was far from being politically sussed.
But was very aware and slightly enraged that over a year ago
we were on a 44-hour week. Then somehow the shipping
companies slipped in a 56-hour week, meaning we worked every
day of the week without a day off for the duration of the trip.
Our demands were for a 40-hour week, not unusual given that
every other British worker was on a 40-hour week. There may
have been other issues with regard to conditions but, the fair
working week was the main item.

So, on the day of the protest march – my only ever protest
march – to Trafalgar Square, I felt like a righteous crusader.
'Of course this is a fair demand,' and the rightful nature of our
strike would be understood by all and sundry. During the
march my political naivety was exposed by first thinking and
then saying to my marching buddies;

'Who the fuck are those whiffy looking people in duffle coats
shouting the odds and dishing out dodgy newspapers? They're
not seamen!'

On arrival at the square there were some rousing speeches
and feelings of comradeship. That's it, that's that sorted. Not so
– we were on strike for almost seven weeks. Lambasted by the
media, noticeably by the then working-class rag, The Daily
Mirror, and the then prime minister Harold Wilson, leader of
the working man's party, for being Commies and bringing the
country to its knees. The strike ended with no change. We had
now achieved a 48-hour week instead of the 40 that we were
demanding, and still four more than it was last year before the

furtive 56-hour week was sprung upon us. A strange Indian bazaar bartering logic that suggests we had made gains, now a six-day working week instead of the seven-day working week.

Not being one for conspiracy theories, it is hard not to acknowledge that some collusion that has been suggested and well documented in the various post-mortems of the strike took place between the government, Shipping Federation, and the Seamen's Union. In essence the weak union hierarchy were battling for survival amidst simmering discontent and had no choice but to call a strike – the union that seemed hand-in-glove with the shipping federation. After all, they allowed the current grievance of a 56-hour week to slip in through the back door a year previously, to the consternation of its members. Now, amid calls for a breakaway union and the spectre of uncontrolled unofficial strike actions being threatened to take place, forced them to call for strike action and placate the growing disenchantment of their members. And by so doing, on the surface, they boosted their credibility and strengthened their positions, cleverly. If the conspiracy theory was justified, along with their bedfellows, the ship owners and government, the union controlled the whole outcome of the strike with just some collateral damage to all concerned. This timely official strike action assured that there would be no fear of long term and more damaging illegal strike actions and disruption that was rightly brewing.

The seamen supporting the strike were confined to a relatively small proportion of the whole membership, consisting of those currently on ships and on leave in the UK, and those that came in during the strike period. All the ships outside of UK waters all over the globe merrily continued on with their normal business without disruption. If there were any threats of walkouts when in foreign ports, then this was not likely to happen, due to a certain apathy and politicised nature of seamen, as well as a lack of communication, courtesy of the radio officer. Whole crews marching down gangways singing 'Keep the red flag flying!' could not be imagined. But if they did attempt some sort of solidarity protests, such as withdrawing labour, they would have been hit with the full weight of the ship's articles that all have signed. The perpetrators could/would immediately be banged up on a charge of 'MUTINY!'

All in all it was a bit of a kicking, and the beginning of the decline of the mercantile marine and British seaman. A maritime tradition, cast adrift. It was claimed that the strike had brought the country to its knees, a load of fanny. The only people on their knees were the seamen.

Thoughtfully, 'The Almighty' decided to let England win the World Cup just a month after the strike ended. All was well again in the blessed Isle of Shareholders.

Running away to sea, running off with the visiting funfair, running off to the circus, running away to join the Foreign Legion, running off to Gretna Green. Today most of the options have run out, nor any way to relieve the pressure valve by knowing there lies a possible exit.

The terrible mortal toll on the defenceless non-combatant, war-time merchant seamen and their vessels, undrilled in dishing out death, a knife and spike for deck work and a packet of Capstan or Woodbine fags for comfort, whilst they frequently anticipated at any moment to be blown to smithereens. A tough hardy stock, a good proportion who'd arrived at sea came via a well-established route, the unloved abandoned clientele of the established orphanages, particularly Dr Barnardo's. As early as 1919, Dr Barnardo had instigated the setting up of a nautical school, to instruct and prepare boys of maturing age for a career and a life at sea. It was well-meaning intentions by those charitable foundations that it would be the making of their charges, orphans with no family support waiting when coming of age. I am sure for most it was their making. Also it suited the shipping companies who funded, to a degree, this facility, in order to obtain ideal fodder readily institutionalised with no family distractions.

Another means of entrance would be by candidates from rural and isolated communities, who were badly paid or with a scarcity of work, and so went to sea and often became the major breadwinner for their dependents. When home on leave, the returning seafarer, though viewed with some mysterious exoticism, it was their tanned re-appearances which also meant – for the pragmatically minded nefarious drinkers in the local pub – that they had a few quid tucked away, and if lucky, were gagging for a booze-up to counter the months of confinement at sea. As night follows day this was often the scenario.

Also as often it is primarily economics and a structured escape that still seduces today, with army recruitment – young boys, oblivious, signing up and still at the age when just eligible to vote, already returning from a first tour of duty minus a limb.

There must be untold romantics from all walks of life who have skinned out to sea, all those characters, the dreams that motivated, the adventures encountered, all never to be documented belonging to the infinity of the vast rich parallel of unrecorded history. To my modest knowledge, those literary worthies who wrote so grandly and famously of having been at sea, managed to dabble for real in just one or two trips at most – as the humble ordinary seaman – hardly experience, but far and enough to spark the senses to fully understand its world.

My only transferable skill from sea to shore was the ability to swing a paint brush. Therefore I gravitated toward decorating work for my money; always intending that it was interim as I was now developing an interest in the creative side of things, getting lost in painting and sculpture, holed up in my version of a Montmartre garret, my little bedroom at home in my parents' council flat.

With much water under the bridge, I still maintained my principled stance. Having pretty much settled into shore life, I thought maybe I had an edge and would not for long be afflicted with perceived aimlessness, dead end jobs, and the lure by association of illegal activities. Having had another prolonged rest from work, and not wanting to stretch my mum's unconditional tolerance for her lovely son, I undertook my usual dispiriting trawl through the Situations Vacant columns of both the Evening News and Standard, skirting the known mind-numbing implications of the various job titles and wage opportunities on offer, when, totally unexpectedly, out jumped the heading 'SEAMEN REQUIRED: non-repatriation ship delivery to Australia'. That was it, the evening papers generally came out before midday so that afternoon I duly arrived in Leadenhall Street, the City, hub of shipping company headquarters, descendants of the grand mercenary ship owners of yesteryear.

With hardly an interview, and just a quick glance at the seaman's passport – The Discharge Book – to see if it was clean, I was taken on. There was no taking chances with DR boys. DR refers to a conduct report that is recorded alongside basic engagement information in one's seaman's book on termination of a voyage. This possible permanent blemish is encompassed in a rubber stamp wielded by the Captain. The following stamps are at his disposal: VG – very good, this is generally handed out and expected. The next stamp is simply; GOOD – which implies the opposite, failure to impress. Whether work-wise, conduct, or behaviour, you have not quite come up to scratch. Another is VNC – voyage not completed. That more often meant you had jumped ship! Another taint – unreliable - affecting your employment expectations. Then the big one: DR – declined to report. To put it mildly, to get one of these you would have to have been a very naughty boy. This stigma on your passport could restrict travel on certain ships with nervy dispositions. But not restrict employment totally. I quite liked the minimal, simplistic abbreviations and lack of detail, for the reasoning for the impervious inked stamp. For me, born of a kind of realistic and pragmatic attitude that once existed, that is almost forgiving and not condemning, almost a Christian redemption at root that acknowledges the harshness and conditions of the seaman and therefore makes allowances for such. A rap on the knuckles and no gory details left room for negotiations with future world weary ship's Captains to overlook this one time, the dreaded glaring DR.

Basically it was an under the counter job, bypassing the inhibitive Shipping Federation and Seamen's Union. The purpose, to not fulfil certain economic commitments. a saving lauded by shareholders as good house-keeping. Non-repatriation meant when the delivered ship arrived at its destination, that was it for you; no flight back home – a requirement if gone through the conventional route. Those high status moral institutions were still playing tricks. However if the destination appealed, or an Antipodean wanted to get home – 'Ideal'.

The crew required was – First Mate, Engineer, Greaser, four Deckhands, one Cook. It was a small, just-built coastal tanker, Faiza, gt 910. Itinerary – fly to Amsterdam, pick up ship and take it to Bahrain in the Persian Gulf. There, pick up deep-sea tug, take to Brisbane, Australia, a two-legged trip. The motley crew – always motley – flew to Amsterdam, the Captain already on board. The Mate, having all the travel documents,

being group leader. He was a pleasant bloke who turned out to be somewhat of an innocent, giving rise to the impression that he may have blown it at some point, having had in the recent past been indiscreet or done something nautically wrong, and now couldn't believe his luck in getting this job that began with the responsibility for getting the crew there intact. He carried a wodge of money for any unexpected expenses.

Among my fellow crew was Geoff, an Aussie who'd been stranded in the UK, a good rough-edged likeable bloke, partial to a drink. His calm, unfazed smiley nature, even when under the influence, due in part to his feral-like upbringing on the fringes of an Aboriginal community, nurtured his nature of constant joy with a healthy anti-establishment attitude. The consequences of taking no bullshit meant numerous run-in's with authority. He seemed to me so right about things, not mad, deluded, half-cocked or a beguiling great intellect. Just an unsuspecting torch-carrier of normal base thinking, someone I would nominate as a representative to meet the aliens if they ever made it down.

Another deck hand was Donald, originally a Scot, but domiciled in New Zealand, again stranded in the UK, after visiting his Scottish connections and now potless. Don was of small wiry build and sported a pugilistic flat nose acquired by many childhood scraps punching above his weight in his native Glasgow. Achieving a belated 'don't mess with me' look, the disarming side of the likeable gregarious 'chirpy chappy' just about masked a confronting pain in the arse. It was surprising that he had survived till now with just a smattering of facial scars and had not been mortally wounded.

Two things stick in my mind about Don. Firstly he was brought up as a child in a Glasgow brothel collectively by the inmates – and was never 100% sure who his mother was – and then subsequently fostered.

Secondly he was, whilst in his early days having done a stint in the army, stationed at Christmas Island in the Pacific Ocean. He witnessed without protection – as has been well documented – a major atom bomb test, the whole mushroom cloud bit on the horizon before his eyes. Two rather disadvantaged events, as well as everything else.

The third member of the deck crowd was around my age, younger than the other two, who was amiable and just a little cagey with dubious deck skills. It was no surprise when toward the end of the trip he turned out to be a nephew of the Captain and lived in the same small farming town as he. I have no strong memories of the two engine room dwellers.

The main man had to be Arthur – the cook – the oldest man of the crew; a real anchor of a character. His last job was cooking in a retirement home in the leafy countryside where really he should have been an inhabitant, regaling the armchair-bound ladies with his shipboard tales, not bobbing up and down on a small boat for weeks on end. Maybe his idea, being oblivious of mortality, was a wholesome life beckoning as cook/sheep shearer in the outback.

On arrival in Amsterdam we had some hiccups, with further travel down the coast to our destination. The result was the whole evening was spent in Amsterdam. This began with a visit to a bar for deserved refreshments after our weary travel. Everyone including the Mate seemed extremely jolly. After a few jars of relaxing Dutch beer and hardly having eaten the Mate announced that we should retire to a restaurant. He was rising to the occasion with his responsibility to the men under his care and after all he had been given money for surely times like this.

The outcome was we were directed to the main restaurant area. There were no snack bars in sight, in case the restaurant idea was reneged on. No chance with the Mate a little tipsy now and flush with his wodge of money. We, with some collective coercing, entered what seemed a rather plush traditional Dutch restaurant. Fantastic food and much wine was polished off; the Mate loving it at the head of the table. His demeanour only changed when the bill was presented.

We finally arrived at the ship late that night – the old man waiting at the top of the gangway. Up until then he was a stranger to all except of course the nephew. He had the sternest of expressions and was obviously displeased with the jolly state of his crew. After a begrudging acknowledgement we got on board and to our new smelling, virgin cabins, most of it wrapped up in plastic, which we were requested not to disturb. No sooner than our bags were put down, there was an almighty commotion up on deck. The old man apoplectically bollocking the Mate, his fellow Officer who he had only just met, with some choice language. On an exchange of formal documents he had then asked the mate for the petty cash that he was carrying (the Captain was a regular deliverer of ships and this was one of his many perks). The Mate's wodge (Captain's perk in reality) had been virtually wiped out. It was not unnoticed that he was in the total doghouse for the whole trip, poor sod.

The trip in itself was an uneventful plod given that for seven weeks we stopped just the once for a day at Walvis Bay, South West Africa and managed a run ashore for a few hours. Not the best of places, red-necked and still in the era of apartheid. On the other hand the time at sea for over three weeks was punctuated with only the very odd glimpse of coast and presented a rare unmolested purity in which to exist. Bare horizons, and never-ending theatre in the skies, an undeniable sense of space and power of the constant scripted swell of the Southern Atlantic Ocean, serenity interrupted only on occasion with a bout of dodgy weather, and fortunately, not during our relative calm passage. An ugly big bastard of a storm that can descend and mug you with its rage, emphasising the sea's volatile range and leave you gibbering with your inconsequence.

So, the prospect of steering the boat that has no automatic steering system, for two four-hour watch periods a day, completely boring, with hardly a corner to turn or deviation to make in the wide 360° expanse was strangely enjoyable during the daylight hours. At night the only light in the darkness, the mesmerising highlights of the compass points, promoted a mind altering battle with the desire to sleep.

During this spell in blissful isolation I must confess to a slight wobbly, due in part to stepping back from my decision to leave the sea, and prompting 'what the fuck am I doing here?' thoughts. I'd been sensitised by artistic pursuits and flowery thoughts whilst ashore, and was now slightly at odds with this occupation. My saviour, having dipped my toe into a dark moment, was Arthur. After his day's toil in the galley on the little after-deck, having a fag and a cup of tea and regaling various stories of his vast ancient past and his obvious genuine pride and pleasure in feeding us all – though mostly plain grub and cooked to death – was lovely, his solid presence was a complete antidote to my malaise.

One little incident that broke the monotony was the Captain's nephew, a big chap, and Don, a little chap, having a full-scale fight on the deck that they were in the process of painting. The nephew could not handle Don, who had also by now unsurprisingly riled the Captain (so maybe official blessing), and Don was definitely not keen on the nephew. The inevitable was not whether but when. Being a little tub there was soon an audience of at least three. We viewed it for a while then broke up the paint-splattered combatants. Don the survivor was the winner on points.

The remaining journey, once rounding the potentially naughty Cape of Good Hope, was another slow plod now entering the Indian Ocean up the west coast of Africa on through to the now no-go area of sea for unprotected shipping along the Kenyan and Somalian coast 'pirate hunting grounds'. Mind you, we would have had Don on board. Then the Gulf of Oman and onto the Persian Gulf, the lands of tyrannical Sheikdom, and lovely street food. On arrival at Bahrain we were informed that the second leg of the journey had fallen through. Unsympathetic terrorists spoilt our travel plans by highjacking two British Airways jets complete with passengers on board, stranded on the runway in sweltering heat while authorities were trying to get together this new phenomenon. One knee-jerk response was a moratorium on most commercial movement that affected our tug being cleared; at least that was what we were told. The outcome was the company was committed to fly us back to the UK. However those who were keen to continue to Oz, including myself, paid the small difference and duly flew into Sydney airport – but not before milking the unexpected pleasure ahead when the shipping agent had no choice at short notice but to put us up in a rather upmarket plush hotel for a couple of days until a semblance of air movement recommenced. To our glee we found that a bar bill was included, long enough for sufficient abuse – before the agent discovered his oversight. This included a memorable afternoon around the hotel pool sharing cocktails with a group of beautiful airhostesses on a break between flights – until an uninhibited and over-active Don became too explicit, and completely spooked them.

Six months or so kicking around Sydney followed. Then itchy feet and off to Melbourne where I managed to track down Geoff for a visit. He had renewed his acquaintance with the Australian Merchant Navy that mainly serviced the southern seas, a highly unionised, highly paid outfit, desirable, and impossible to break into. So my idle remark to Geoff, 'What's the chances of joining an Aussie ship?' was greeted with mirth. 'You're fucking joking mate!' He did concede there might be an outside chance of casual work in Melbourne docks working by on ships that were in port. Because of brilliant working conditions, Aussie seaman once in port were off on paid leave, unlike the 24/7 containment of their British counterparts.

A humid evening was spent caning a number of tinnies at Geoff's abode in an edgy suburb of ageing timber board houses, as Geoff's conviviality attracted sporadic visits from the favela's restless. Finally the morning arrived, and off we go to pay a visit to the union rep, amiable influential Jacko – the Don in the docks. Geoff introduced me as his 'Pommie mate – but alright' who he had shipped out with in the UK.

'Any chance of him getting a bit of casual around the docks, maybe working by?' asked Geoff in a speculative manner, fully expecting the retort, 'Sorry mate, no chance.' Instead, 'He can ship out if he likes,' came the reply from Jacko. 'What!?' Geoff was more taken aback than me, mouthing 'You jammy bugger'. It happened to be the perfect moment. There was an old iron ore carrier belonging to BHP (the Broken Hill Proprietary mining company) about to sail short of a Deckhand, being perceived a bit of a beast of a ship it was being given a wide berth by the choosy Deckies who may have been available. So, signing on the dotted line, I was now in the luxurious Australian Merchant Service. Wallop!

I joined the ship in Newcastle, New South Wales. Itinerary – out westward across the Great Australian Bight heading for the isolated north-west coast towns of Dampier and Port Headland, two iron ore mining towns. Red-earthed, red-hot, and red-necked, no wonder there was a reluctance. Fortunately there was a semblance of air-conditioning on the ship. If you walked up on deck it was like entering a sauna 120°+. The ship, then returning carrying on around north then Eastern Australia through the Great Barrier Reef and back to Newcastle, so circumnavigating Oz.

Good points were visiting my cousin who recently emigrated, chasing the money her husband had landed a job in hell, an iron ore furnace in Dampier. I surprised them with a visit carrying a case of a much prized Sydney brew, Resch's beer 'the best', and not available in Hades town. As a Pommie warm beer drinker I fully understood now the Aussie preference for ice cold beer.

The little known obscure town of Dampier was named after one of England's greatest seafarers, explorer, navigator and hydrographer, three times circumnavigator of the world and the first Englishman to explore and describe the Australian coast – eighty years before Cook. William Dampier, a man lost in history and almost totally unknown to the general public, his achievements were phenomenal and should rank him up there alongside if not above Captain Cook and all the other worthies who are lapped up in our history books.

His observational and scientific inquiry led to his revolutionary discourse of winds, tides and currents that became the definitive invaluable bible for future sea-farers including Cook, and required study for all midshipmen in Lord Nelson's navy.

An obsessive curiosity for the natural world led to careful, detailed, and objective recording of all around him, a pioneer in what is now referred to as descriptive botany and zoology, the first to record and describe many discoveries ranging from the avocado pear to the effects of marijuana. Dampier's observations led to suggestions of location-dependent differences within species and led to Charles Darwin referencing his works when formulating his theory of natural selection. A map maker par excellence of incredible accuracy; this and much more all undertaken during the last quarter of the seventeenth century, not as one might expect by a venerable scientific scholar of the day, but, by a Somerset farmer's boy of rudimentary education, whilst for most part, due to circumstances, plying the trade of a buccaneer'. The reason for his absence in the Hall of Fame.

If it were pure piracy, the same activity as 'plundering ships on the high seas', it would more likely to have had official blessing and seal of approval of the country under which flag the ship was flying and generally commissioned for that sole purpose. He then would have been lauded to the rafters.

Buccaneers however were a collection of waifs and strays of the sea, without allegiances, indiscriminately pursuing pots of gold, mostly refugees of harsh regimes, hardened survivors fallen upon and embracing the free spirited nature and comradeship of the collective of outlaws. One cannot imagine a more frightening group of individuals. Surprisingly they kept an orderly house and were very democratic with their decision making. Electing by vote the Captain or Commander, and, accepting the autonomy necessary for the role, also garnered pragmatically punishments agreed upon to be essential for order and moral.

Then off to work, crazed pirates, bravely bonkers, raiding anything of worth, chasing down sails on the horizon, sacking and pillaging coastal towns, marching on wealthy cities, experiencing deprivation and elation, acting viciously and humanly, death ever present. This environment was William Dampier's work place where he made his contributions to civilisation.

THE IRON ORE CARRIER

On board this ship was the usual interesting ensemble. The first day on board, a union meeting was called by the large hirsute Bosun, top of the agenda, to complain about the absence of lollies (sweets), the trip before. I liked it!

Whether we were tied up or at sea, every Friday without fail we were paid wages in cash, a fistful of Aussie dollars. Single berth accommodation, and a fully filled fridge of goodies on tap in the seamen's mess and no need to work overtime, meant the consumption of beer more likely. I'd made a decision at the onset not to drink and get too involved with the crowd. By now I had got to a point where I wanted to leave Australia behind me and exorcise my remaining wanderlust. Now with the opportunity of some well paid work it was possible. Eight months or so of hand-to-mouth, and a natural inability, certainly when there is not much surplus, to being able to save meant I could have been stuck for some time, so, determined not to blow it and suppressing my gregarious instincts, not a drop passed my lips for the whole trip. The misconception of thinking I'd be taken for some odd bastard when declaring I didn't drink (and a Pom! to boot) was unfounded. I was one of the crowd.

Every Friday I would retrieve the envelope secreted in my cabin which had SOUTH AMERICA wrote on it in bold letters and would deposit my fistful of dollars neatly alongside the previous week's stash, monies that could easily have been squandered if bevvying with the chaps, and the inevitable gambling sessions that erupted now and again.

I was so proud of myself.

I had a naive plan. To visit my favourite place, South America, starting in Chile and hence a meander through the whole continent to Central America a little stopover in Cuba, a mooch through Mexico... USA... Canada... Blah... blah... blah.

On arrival in Newcastle and pay-off day I announced to some of the chaps I was leaving Oz, and, by implication, the position I now had as a made man in the perfect job for a working man. You must be 'effing bonkers' was their response, almost as if I had slighted them by turning my back so soon; understandable, for if I was in Oz as a serious migrant this would be Utopia. The pay and conditions were phenomenal. For every 9 months on Articles, you got 5 months paid leave, you could quite easily acquire a car (a big old Holden), house and pool, the migrant's dream. Then a little later, a boat to go cray-fishing during days languishing on leave. I did consider for a moment, then thought no, sod that I'm off!

I assumed to get to Chile from Australia would be quite easy, both being in the lower bit of the world. But it wasn't, at least by sea. There were two direct sailings to Chile from Oz; neither dates near enough to wait for. I was up for immediate departure. The option that I took was to book a berth on a passenger ship that was heading back to Europe, stop off on route at Tahiti then connect with a flight from there to Santiago, a stay in Tahiti for three days before the connection was made, sounded good. Back to sea as a passenger.

I was the only person to disembark from the huge liner. Having the cheapest berth meant sharing with two others, a Portuguese and a German going back to Europe; both adventurous characters who'd exhausted, for different reasons, what was on offer to them in Australia. We, for this moment in our lives, had entered that transient age old world of going forth optimistically or returning less so. They were envious of my continuing possibilities, unlike them, pacified and being transported back home. Gushing about my plans albeit naïve and ill considered and disembarking in Tahiti touched a raw nerve. They wanted to come along as if I were a team leader of an exotic expedition, but logistically in many ways as much as they tried, it was an impossibility. Again standing on the little dock in Papeete, the sun slowly dipping on the horizon, I solitarily waved off the big ship and my new found envious mates, little knowing that I would not be long behind them and on my way home.

The cheery Customs officer who checked me in and looked at my onward travel details, plane ticket etc, momentarily put on a stern expression and said, 'You had better get on that plane when it arrives.'

'Well, yea, course, I'm off to South America!' Fully into my seasoned worldly traveller mode. He then went back to cheery,

'Ok! Aloha! Welcome to Tahiti, enjoy your stay.'

Apparently, I discovered later, like a frequent unwanted pest, there is a constant stream of adventurous lone chaps who think it is an original idea to turn up in Tahiti and wander off into the exotic interior to live happily ever after in paradise, hopefully hand in hand with a Tahitian beauty. The result was half-starved idealists being retrieved from the undergrowth.

I did have one fleeting Tahitian moment, after procuring a room in a cheap guesthouse. In the adjoining room – they were more like flimsy cubicles – was a French marine on R&R (rest and recuperation) who kindly took pity on the lost non-French-speaking soul in the next room and invited me along with his buddies to the 'in the know' hot spot.

A large palm-fringed partially outdoor club just hidden from the general tourist trade with a stage and dance floor, the highlight of the early evening show that accounted for the large contingent of French squaddies was specially imported from Paris. A sophisticated burlesque act, basically a stripper, performing an updated version of the dance of the seven veils that followed a ventriloquist with a line in blueish French jokes. Then, show over and the squaddies were placated with some homely French culture. Tahitian music and dancing commenced.

It was then I had my moment so fleeting to be forgotten but for the intensity of that short moment in time. A lovely Tahitian girl had approached my table where I sat nursing my beer solitarily absorbing the exotica all around, leant forward warmly smiling and placed a flower in my hair. I must have had a look of panic. Not having a clue what she had said I muttered something back, producing a puzzled look in return. Then my French multi-lingual mate having observed the encounter was by my side with a nudge in the ribs, 'Mon ami, eez ze zign zat she likes vou and would like to dance.' So, no choice. On my feet and hand in hand we walked to the dance floor, she still smiling but probably wondering what planet I had come from. Especially now initial panic had momentarily morphed into sheer panic. But soon I was into this weird dance and finally relaxed as a result of the few beers I'd had, and the moment. Part of the traditional dance of swaying rhythmically? Feet slightly parted, knees bent and a furious knocking of the knees together in accompaniment with the rhythmic drumming – more like the sound of two lumps of hard wood banging together – whilst grinning inanely and looking inelegant. That image was my Tahitian moment of communing with the men of the Bounty. Needless to say regretting my lack of French, just smiles between us, nothing became of my fleeting encounter.

Finally my departure time arrived, midnight in the deserted airport. One of two passengers embarking, destination Santiago, stopping just once en-route at Easter Island. I was unaware that that was certainly to be one of the most fascinating mysterious and isolated destinations that one could have the privilege to visit; a total surprise, expecting just a fuel stop on some ordinary island in the mid Pacific. Not that they are at all ordinary. Just that Easter Island was extraordinary, an eighth wonder of the world. And at the beginning of the seventies it was not yet quite geared up as a regular tourist destination that it has subsequently become.

Hence for the duration of a couple of hour stay passengers disembarked and those willing were invited to clamber up on to a couple of ancient opened back lorries that took us on a free round tour of the fascinating, somewhat barren island. It was completely bizarrely dotted with huge four-metre stone sculptures all duplicated with the same likeness, erect, half erect, and others fallen in such great numbers creating a surreal incomprehensible magical scene and the obvious, Why? How?

Answers emerged slowly only after many years of intrigue and investigation by many. The island, although looking the worse for wear and arid, was once a fertile paradise discovered and settled by nomadic seafaring Polynesians who may have been dispossessed due to internecine aggro, falling upon an island that was many hundreds of miles from their homelands at a time of minimal navigation skills. It was just sheer plunging into the unknown to perish, if they had not miraculously come across this microscopic spot in the middle of the desolated South Pacific Ocean. The men women and children were in sufficient numbers to establish a thriving community in a virgin Garden of Eden. The sad story of its subsequent demise and decline to its current tree-less state over many hundreds of years is almost a microcosmic analogy of our present globe. Power struggles, domination, greed, non-co-operation and finally eating themselves out of house and home.

Their occupation throughout this period interjected with the sheer mindless toil by generation after generation quarrying huge identical stone sculptures. These were basically a featureless long elongated yet stylised face with long nose and distinctive long drooping ears, no respite or relief from the monotonous relentless activity, primitively carving by hand direct from the rock face in some kind of idolatrous servitude. A present-day affliction still. Then the monumental task of manoeuvring two to three tons of solid stone to different parts of the island and then planting them in an erect state so as to be staring out at the empty sea.

On arrival at Santiago airport, which sits just outside the city, I shared a cab with a fellow passenger into the central area of Santiago. The road passed through a vast landscape of a low-level shanty-town, in sharp contrast to the high rise city that we were approaching. Having discovered my left leanings, yet still somewhat naïve, I expected to find a heady mildly revolutionary exciting party atmosphere to get caught up in. A year or so before, Salvador Allende had been the first ever democratically elected communist president, which unfortunately, in hindsight, meant he had no reason to shoot the opposition as Castro readily did. The consequences were the old order were left to fester in their opulent abodes while the slow-burning change as yet not materialising fostered a depressed atmosphere ripe for the paranoid US and the sneaky bastard CIA to infiltrate and manage the downfall of Allende. He was replaced by the strutting, pompous, right-wing dictator Pinochet, who orchestrated the demise of vast numbers of decent human beings, extinguishing yet again the hope of self determination.

I survived about five days of aimless wanderings, acutely aware of my shortcomings, no Spanish or Portuguese, low on money, no traveling companion to boost moral and no anti-imperialist murals to lend a hand in painting.

I was by now seriously missing my five-year-old nephew. That was it, sod it! I was off. I booked a flight home the following morning. That left me about twenty dollars in change, out of my dwindling stash of cash, confident that I was just popping back home and would come back later and resume my travels...

After a short stopover in Argentina, whereupon everyone onboard was photographed disembarking the plane for the hour or two stay in the airport lounge, this seemed especially sinister given that it was nighttime and it was flash photography.

The journey was quite a long haul until finally in bright sunshine we were descending, the vivid green of the fields below, land of the free. Blighty lay before us. I made a rare flag-waving emotional connection, proud even, 'Home!', a physical illusory moment that somehow previously had always been sullied by empire plundering and the last night of the Proms. Occupiers apart, the terrain of that little island was unique, minimal adversity, lush and fertile, with the sea its only borders.

I'd been away for over a year, and enjoyed the euphoric state of re-uniting, and for a short while – too short – the status of a minor celebrity. Tales told and tales listened to soon wore thin. No longer in transit, the ordinariness of work – money – residing beginning to overwhelm. I found myself once again trooping down to the docks and re-engaging. And on a cold, cold winter's day made the error of joining the first available ship. Off to Norway and the icy fjords instead of sensible, warm climes. Dark, cold and grim, although spectacular, I'd done a 'wrong un' and was now determined when back to call it a day.

ABOUT THE AUTHOR

Mick Hugo was born in 1946 in Hoxton, in the East End
of London. He grew up with his mother, a dressmaker, his father,
a demolition worker, and his sister. At 15 he joined the Merchant
Navy and left during the 1966 Seamen's Strike. He rejoined as
a casual, finally leaving in 1972.

Mick became a painter and decorator, then a general builder.
He is a self-taught painter, sculptor and illustrator.

His wife died in 1999, he has three children and six grandchildren.
He still works as a builder and lives in the East End.

Skinning Out —— To Sea
by Mick Hugo

Published by Bowline Books 2016
www.bowlinebooks.com

All illustrations by Mick Hugo © 2016

Copyright Mick Hugo © 2016
All rights reserved.

ISBN 978-0-9934295-0-7

Designed by Sam Blunden

Set in Doves Type. Created by Robert Green using
sources from original Doves Press publications and
metal sorts recovered from the River Thames by
Robert Green and the Port of London Authority
salvage team. www.dovestype.com

Printed in London by XtraPrint

With thanks to Juliet Ash, Ken Worpole, Robert Hanks,
Joe Pipal and Sam Blunden